The Changeling

By
Thomas Middleton &
William Rowley

ANODOS BOOKS
Candida Casa

Thomas Middleton (1580-1627) & William Rowley (1585-1626)
Originally published in 1652
Editing, cover, and internal design by Alisdair MacNoravaich for Anodos Books.
Copyright © 2017 Anodos Books. All rights reserved.

Anodos Books
1c Kings Road
Whithorn
Newton Stewart
Dumfries & Galloway
DG8 8PP

Contents

DRAMATIS PERSONAE.

Vermandero, father to Beatrice
Tomazo de Piracquo, a noble lord[1]
Alonzo de Piracquo, his brother, suitor to Beatrice
Alsemero, a nobleman, afterwards married to Beatrice
Jasperino, his friend
Alibius, a jealous doctor[2]
Lollio, his man
Pedro, friend to Antonio
Antonio, the changeling
Franciscus, the counterfeit madman[3]
Deflores, servant to Vermandero[4]
Madmen
Two Servants to Alsemero
A Servant to Vermandero
Beatrice[5] [Joanna[6]], daughter to Vermandero
Diaphanta, her waiting woman[7]
Isabella, wife to Alibius[8]

The Scene: Alicant[9]

---

[1]Daalder cites William Power, "Middleton's Way with Names," *Notes & Queries* 205 (1960) regarding the reasoning for certain character names; some of the following interpretations are more convincing than others: e.g., "Tomazo" may allude to a doubting Thomas.

[2]"he who is elsewhere"

[3]"Frenchman, a free and thus licentious man"

[4]"deflowerer"

[5]"she who makes happy"

[6]"the Lord's grace"

[7]"the diaphanous one," or, "the red hot one"

[8]"God has sworn," "yellowish white," *bella* = beauty

[9]Alicante is a port on the east coast of Spain, 75 miles south of Valencia.

ACT I.

SCENE I.

A street near the harbor.

Enter Alsemero.

Als. 'Twas in the temple where I first beheld her,
And now again the same; what omen yet
Follows of that? None but imaginary.
Why should my hopes or fate be timorous?
The place is holy, so is my intent:
I love her beauties to the holy purpose,[10]
And that methinks admits comparison
With man's first creation, the place blest,[11]
And is his right home back, if he achieve it.
The church hath first begun our interview
And that's the place must join us into one,
So there's beginning and perfection[12] too.

Enter Jasperino.

Jas. O sir, are you here? Come, the wind's fair with you;
Y'are like to have a swift and pleasant passage.

Als. Sure y'are deceiv'd, friend; 'tis contrary
In my best judgment.

Jas. What, for Malta?
If you could buy a gale amongst the witches,[13]
They could not serve you such a lucky pennyworth[14]
As comes a' God's name.[15]

Als. Even now I observ'd

---

[10]Marriage.

[11]The Garden of Eden, Paradise.

[12]I.e., a perfect circle. This heavenly image is juxtaposed to the barley-break circle of hell which ultimately circumscribes them.

[13]Witches could supposedly influence the weather; cf. *The Witch* I.ii, *Macbeth* I.iii, Webster and Rowley's *A Cure for a Cuckold* IV. ii.

[14]Bargain.

[15]In God's name, freely, as opposed to the witches' bargain.

3

The temple's vane[16] to turn full in my face;
I know 'tis against me.

Jas. Against you?
Then you know not where you are.

Als. Not well indeed.

Jas. Are you not well, sir?

Als. Yes, Jasperino,
Unless there be some hidden malady
Within me that I understand not.

Jas. And that
I begin to doubt, sir; I never knew
Your inclinations to travels at a pause
With any cause to hinder it till now.
Ashore you were wont to call your servants up,
And help to trap your horses for the speed.
At sea I have seen you weigh the anchor with 'em,
Hoist sails for fear to lose the foremost breath,
Be in continual prayers for fair winds;
And have you chang'd your orisons?[17]

Als. No, friend,
I keep the same church, same devotion.

Jas. Lover I'm sure y'are none: the stoic[18]
Was found in you long ago; your mother
Nor best friends, who have set snares of beauty,
Ay, and choice ones too, could never trap you that way.
What might be the cause?

Als. Lord, how violent
Thou art: I was but meditating of
Somewhat I heard within the temple.

Jas. Is this violence? 'Tis but idleness
Compar'd with your haste yesterday.

---

[16]Weather-vane, a symbol of changeability.

[17]Prayers.

[18]One who represses passions and emotions, from the ancient philosophical school of Athens founded by Zeno.

4

Als. I'm all this while a-going, man.

Enter Two Servants [*to* Alsemero].

Jas. Backwards, I think, sir. Look, your servants.

1st Serv. The seamen call; shall we board your trunks?

Als. No, not today.

Jas. 'Tis the critical day,
It seems, and the sign in Aquarius.[19]

2nd Serv. We must not to sea today; this smoke will bring forth fire.[20]

Als. Keep all on shore; I do not know the end,
Which needs I must do, of an affair in hand
Ere I can go to sea.

1st Serv. Well, your pleasure.

2nd Serv. [*Aside to First Servant*] Let him e'en take his leisure too; we are
safer on land.

[*Exeunt* Alsemero's Servants. *Enter* Beatrice, Diaphanta, *and* Servants.
[Alsemero *bows to* Beatrice *and kisses her.*

Jas. [*Aside*] How now! The laws of the Medes[21] are chang'd sure: salute a
woman! He kisses too: wonderful! Where learnt he this? And does it
perfectly too; in my conscience he ne'er rehears'd it before. Nay, go on,
this will be stranger and better news at Valencia than if he had
ransom'd half Greece from the Turk![22]

Bea. You are a scholar, sir.

Als. A weak one, lady.

Bea. Which of the sciences is this love you speak of?

Als. From your tongue I take it to be music.

Bea. You are skillful in't, can sing at first sight. [23]

---

[19]The Water-Carrier, hence favorable for a sea voyage.

[20]Proverbial: "Where there's smoke, there's fire."

[21]Unchangeable laws (Daniel 6.8).

[22]Greece was part of the Ottoman Empire from 1460 to 1830.

[23]1) sight-read music, 2) vow love at the first meeting; cf. *Troilus and Cressida* V. ii.

Als. And I have show'd you all my skill at once.
I want more words to express me further
And must be forc'd to repetition:
I love you dearly.

Bea. Be better advis'd, sir:
Our eyes are sentinels unto our judgments,
And should give certain judgment what they see;
But they are rash sometimes, and tell us wonders
Of common things, which when our judgments find,
They can then check the eyes, and call them blind.

Als. But I am further, lady; yesterday
Was mine eyes' employment, and hither now
They brought my judgment, where are both agreed.
Both houses[24] then consenting, 'tis agreed,
Only there wants the confirmation
By the hand royal; that's your part, lady.

Bea. Oh, there's one above me,[25] sir. [*Aside*] For five days past[26]
To be recall'd! Sure, mine eyes were mistaken;
This was the man was meant me. That he should come
So near his time, and miss it!

Jas. [*Aside*] We might have come by the carriers from Valencia, I see,
and sav'd all our sea-provision: we are at farthest[27] sure. Methinks I
should do something too; I meant to be a venturer[28] in this voyage.
Yonder's another vessel: I'll board her; if she be lawful prize,[29] down
goes her topsail![30]

Enter Deflores.

Def. Lady, your father--

---

[24]An allusion to the Houses of Parliament, Lords and Commons, representing sight and judgment.

[25]If Beatrice is the sovereign (the "hand royal" that makes a Parliamentary bill a law), then the authority above her is her father, or God.

[26]Beatrice was engaged to Alonzo five days before.

[27]At the limits of the journey.

[28]One who takes a share in the risks and expenses of a commercial voyage and receives a share of the profits in return; cf. *The Phoenix* II. i.

[29]A vessel which may legally be captured.

[30]A sign of a ship's surrender.

Bea. Is in health, I hope.

Def. Your eye shall instantly instruct you, lady.
He's coming hitherward.

Bea. What needed then
Your duteous preface? I had rather
He had come unexpected; you must stall
A good presence with unnecessary blabbing:
And how welcome for your part you are,
I'm sure you know.

Def. [*Aside*] Will't never mend, this scorn,
One side nor other?[31] Must I be enjoin'd
To follow still whilst she flies from me? Well,
Fates do your worst, I'll please myself with sight
Of her, at all opportunities,
If but to spite her anger. I know she had
Rather see me dead than living, and yet
She knows no cause for't but a peevish will.

Als. You seem'd displeas'd, lady, on the sudden.

Bea. Your pardon, sir, 'tis my infirmity,
Nor can I other reason render you
Than his or hers, of some particular thing
They must abandon as a deadly poison,
Which to a thousand other tastes were wholesome;
Such to mine eyes is that same fellow there,
The same that report speaks of the basilisk.[32]

Als. This is a frequent frailty in our nature;
There's scarce a man amongst a thousand sound
But hath his imperfection: one distastes
The scent of roses, which to infinites[33]
Most pleasing is and odoriferous.
One oil,[34] the enemy of poison,
Another wine, the cheerer of the heart,

---

[31]One way or another.

[32]In legend, a reptile whose breath and look were thought to be fatal; it was supposed to look somewhat like a lizard, have black and yellow skin and fiery red eyes, and be hatched by a serpent from a cock's egg. Cf. *Cymbeline* II.iv, *The Winter's Tale* I.ii, *2 Henry VI* III.ii, *3 Henry VI* III.ii. Illustration from Edward Topsell's *The History of Serpents*(1608); "basilisk" is Greek for "king," hence the crown.

[33]An infinite number of people.

And lively refresher of the countenance.[35]
Indeed this fault, if so it be, is general:
There's scarce a thing but is both lov'd and loath'd;
Myself, I must confess, have the same frailty.

Bea. And what may be your poison, sir? I am bold with you.

Als. What might be your desire perhaps, a cherry.[36]

Bea. I am no enemy to any creature
My memory has but yon gentleman.

Als. He does ill to tempt your sight, if he knew it.

Bea. He cannot be ignorant of that, sir;
I have not spar'd to tell him so, and I want[37]
To help myself, since he's a gentleman
In good respect with my father and follows him.

Als. He's out of his place then now.

Jas. I am a mad wag, wench.

Dia. So methinks; but for your comfort I can tell you we have a doctor in the city that undertakes the cure of such.

Jas. Tush, I know what physic is best for the state of mine own body.

Dia. 'Tis scarce a well-govern'd state, I believe.

Jas. I could show thee such a thing with an ingredient that we two would compound[38] together, and if it did not tame the maddest blood i' th' town for two hours after, I'll ne'er profess physic[39] again.

Dia. A little poppy,[40] sir, were good to cause you sleep.

---

[34]A medical unction.

[35]Cf. Psalm 104:15, "And wine that maketh glad the heart of man, and oil to make his face to shine...".

[36]This sentence begins with "And" in the Quarto, which was probably accidentally repeated from the previous line; otherwise Alsemero would be answering a question with a question, although one could play him as being evasive here.

[37]Lack means.

[38]With sexual innuendo; cf. "pounded" in III. iii.

[39]Medical science.

[40]Opium.

8

Jas. Poppy! I'll give thee a pop i' th' lips for that first, and begin there.
[*He kisses her.*] Poppy is one simple[41] indeed, and cuckoo, what you
call't,[42] another: I'll discover[43] no more now; another time I'll show thee
all.

Enter Vermandero *and* Servants.

Bea. My father, sir.

Ver. Oh, Joanna, I came to meet thee.
Your devotion's ended?

Bea. For this time, sir.
[*Aside*] I shall change my saint,[44] I fear me: I find
A giddy turning in me.--Sir, this while
I am beholding to this gentleman
Who left his own way to keep me company,
And in discourse I find him much desirous
To see your castle: he hath deserv'd it, sir,
If ye please to grant it.

Ver. With all my heart, sir.
Yet there's an article between:[45] I must know
Your country. We use not to give survey
Of our chief strengths to strangers; our citadels
Are plac'd conspicuous to outward view
On promonts'[46] tops, but within are secrets.

Als. A Valencian, sir.

Ver. A Valencian?
That's native, sir; of what name, I beseech you?

Als. Alsemero, sir.

Ver. Alsemero? Not the son

---

[41]Medicinal herb.

[42]1) the cuckoo-pint, or wild arum; Rowley has noted its phallic shape in *All's Lost by Lust* III.
iii ("those long upright things that grow a yard [slang for penis] above the ground"). 2) The
ladies' smock, another variety of cuckoo flower, traditionally a cure for madness. Also cf. *King
Lear* IV. iv.

[43]Reveal, with the bawdy innuendo.

[44]From the heavenly one of the church to an earthly one in Alsemero; cf. "lips' saint" in V. iii.

[45]Pre-condition.

[46]Promontories'.

Of John de Alsemero?

Als. The same, sir.

Ver. My best love bids you welcome.

Bea. [Aside] He was wont
To call me so, and then he speaks a most
Unfeigned truth.

Ver. Oh, sir, I knew your father.
We two were in acquaintance long ago
Before our chins were worth iulan down,[47]
And so continued till the stamp of time
Had coin'd us into silver. Well, he's gone;
A good soldier went with him.

Als. You went together[48] in that, sir.

Ver. No, by Saint Jaques,[49] I came behind him;
Yet I have done somewhat too. An unhappy day
Swallowed him at last at Gibraltar
In fight with those rebellious Hollanders,[50]
Was it not so?

Als. Whose death I had reveng'd,
Or followed him in fate, had not the late league
Prevented me.

Ver. Ay, ay, 'twas time to breath.
Oh, Joanna, I should ha' told thee news:
I saw Piracquo lately.

Bea. [Aside] That's ill news.

Ver. He's hot preparing for this day of triumph;
Thou must be a bride within this sevennight.

---

[47]The first growth of beard, coined from the name of Aeneas's young son, Iulus Ascanius (*Aeneid* I), itself derived from the Greek ioulos, first growth of beard.

[48]Were his equal.

[49]St. James the Greater, the patron saint of Spain.

[50]The Netherlands, under the dominion of Spain at this time, defeated them in the Battle of Gibraltar on April 25, 1607. On April 8, 1609, the Treaty of the Hague ("the late league") began a twelve-year truce; Spain had been suffering defeats elsewhere, and therefore desired peace ("'twas time to breathe").

Als. [*Aside*] Ha!

Bea. Nay, good sir, be not so violent; with speed
I cannot render satisfaction
Unto the dear companion of my soul,
Virginity, whom I thus long have liv'd with,
And part with it so rude and suddenly,
Can such friends divide never to meet again
Without a solemn farewell?

Ver. Tush, tush, there's a toy.[51]

Als. [*Aside*] I must now part, and never meet again
With any joy on earth.--Sir, your pardon,
My affairs call on me.

Ver. How, sir? By no means;
Not chang'd so soon, I hope? You must see my castle
And her best entertainment ere we part;
I shall think myself unkindly us'd else.
Come, come, let's on; I had good hope your stay
Had been a while with us in Alicant;
I might have bid you to my daughter's wedding.

Als. [*Aside*] He means to feast me, and poisons me beforehand.--
I should be dearly glad to be there, sir,
Did my occasions suit as I could wish.

Bea. I shall be sorry if you be not there
When it is done, sir, but not so suddenly.

Ver. I tell you, sir, the gentleman's complete,
A courtier and a gallant, enrich'd
With many fair and noble ornaments;
I would not change him for a son-in-law
For any he in Spain, the proudest he,
And we have great ones, that you know.

Als. He's much
Bound to you, sir.

Ver. He shall be bound to me,
As fast as this tie can hold him; I'll want
My will else.

---

[51]Trifle.

11

Bea. [*Aside*] I shall want mine if you do it.

Ver. But come, by the way I'll tell you more of him.

Als. [*Aside*] How shall I dare to venture in his castle
When he discharges murderers[52] at the gate?
But I must on, for back I cannot go.

Bea. [*Aside*] Not this serpent[53] gone yet?

Ver. Look, girl, thy glove's fall'n;[54]
Stay, stay, Deflores, help a little.

Def. Here, lady.

[*He hands* Beatrice *her glove.*

Bea. Mischief on your officious forwardness;
Who bade you stoop? They touch my hand no more:
There, for t'other's sake I part with this;
Take 'em and draw thine own skin off with 'em.

[*Exeunt. Manet* Deflores.

Def. Here's a favour come with a mischief: now
I know she had rather wear my pelt tann'd
In a pair of dancing pumps than I should
Thrust my fingers into her sockets[55] here.
I know she hates me, yet cannot choose but love her:
No matter, if but to vex her, I'll haunt her still;
Though I get nothing else, I'll have my will.

[*Exit.*

SCENE II.

A room in Alibius's house.

Enter Alibius *and* Lollio.

Ali. Lollio, I must trust thee with a secret,

---

[52]Small cannon loaded with grapeshot; the word is ironically foreshadowing.

[53]Deflores, continuing the Garden of Eden imagery.

[54]Probably dropped as a token of love for Alsemero, although Daalder sees it as Beatrice's unconscious sexual invitation to Deflores. The blocking possibilities revealing whatever motive she has are numerous.

[55]Finger-holes of the glove, with the sexual innuendo.

12

But thou must keep it.

Lol. I was ever close to a secret, sir.

Ali. The diligence that I have found in thee,
The care and industry already past,
Assures me of thy good continuance.
Lollio, I have a wife.

Lol. Fie, sir, 'tis too late to keep her secret; she's known to be married all the town and country over.

Ali. Thou goest too fast, my Lollio: that knowledge
I allow no man can be barr'd it;
But there is a knowledge which is nearer,
Deeper and sweeter, Lollio.

Lol. Well, sir, let us handle that between you and I.

Ali. 'Tis that I go about man; Lollio,
My wife is young.

Lol. So much the worse to be kept secret, sir.

Ali. Why, now thou meet'st the substance of the point:
I am old, Lollio.

Lol. No, sir, 'tis I am old Lollio.

Ali. Yet why may not this concord and sympathize?
Old trees and young plants often grow together,
Well enough agreeing.

Lol. Ay, sir, but the old trees raise themselves higher and broader than the young plants.[56]

Ali. Shrewd application: there's the fear, man.
I would wear my ring on my own finger;[57]
Whilst it is borrowed it is none of mine,
But his that useth it.

Lol. You must keep it on still then; if it but lie by, one or other will be

---

[56]I.e., by the cuckold's horns.

[57]With the sexual puns on vagina and penis; cf. *Your Five Gallants* II. iv, *The Family of Love* II. iv, *The Merchant of Venice* V. i. This is a comic version of an issue treated seriously later regarding Alonzo's ring.

13

thrusting into't.

Ali. Thou conceiv'st me, Lollio; here thy watchful eye
Must have employment. I cannot always be at home.

Lol. I dare swear you cannot.

Ali. I must look out.

Lol. I know't, you must look out, 'tis every man's case.[58]

Ali. Here I do say must thy employment be.
To watch her treadings, and in my absence
Supply my place.[59]

Lol. I'll do my best, sir; yet surely I cannot see who you should have
cause to be jealous of.

Ali. Thy reason for that, Lollio? 'Tis a comfortable question.

Lol. We have but two sorts of people in the house,[60] and both under the
whip, that's fools and madmen; the one has not wit enough to be
knaves, and the other not knavery enough to be fools.

Ali. Ay, those are all my patients, Lollio.
I do profess the cure of either sort:
My trade, my living 'tis, I thrive by it.
But here's the care that mixes with my thrift:[61]
The daily visitants[62] that come to see
My brainsick patients I would not have
To see my wife. Gallants I do observe
Of quick, enticing eyes, rich in habits,
Of stature and proportion very comely:
These are most shrewd[63] temptations, Lollio.

Lol. They may be easily answered, sir. If they come to see the fools and
madmen, you and I may serve the turn, and let my mistress alone; she's
of neither sort.

---

[58]With the pun on vagina.

[59]With the unintended sexual implication, which later Lollio attempts to realize.

[60]Fools were born simple-minded, madmen went insane later in life.

[61]Profit.

[62]Citizens often visited madhouses for entertainment.

[63]Wicked, mischievous.

14

Ali. 'Tis a good ward.[64] Indeed, come they to see
Our madmen or our fools; let 'em see no more
Than what they come for. By that consequent[65]
They must not see her. I'm sure she's no fool.

Lol. And I'm sure she's no madman.

Ali. Hold that buckler[66] fast, Lollio; my trust
Is on thee, and I account it firm and strong.
What hour is't, Lollio?

Lol. Towards belly hour, sir.

Ali. Dinner time? Thou mean'st twelve a' clock.

Lol. Yes, sir, for every part has his hour. We wake at six and look about us, that's eye hour; at seven we should pray, that's knee hour; at eight walk, that's leg hour; at nine gather flowers, and pluck a rose,[67] that's nose hour; at ten we drink, that's mouth hour; at eleven lay about[68] us for victuals, that's hand hour; at twelve go to dinner, that's belly hour.

Ali. Profoundly, Lollio; it will be long
Ere all thy scholars learn this lesson, and
I did look to have a new one entered. Stay,
I think my expectation is come home.

Enter Pedro *and* Antonio *like an idiot.*

Ped. Save you, sir, my business speaks itself;
This sight takes off the labour of my tongue.

Ali. Ay, ay, sir,
'Tis plain enough, you mean him for my patient.

Ped. [*Giving Alibius money*] And if your pains prove but commodious,[69]
To give but some little strength to his sick
And weak part of nature in him, these are
But patterns to show you of the whole pieces
That will follow to you, beside the charge

---

[64]A defensive position in fencing.

[65]Conclusion.

[66]A small, round shield.

[67]Urinate.

[68]Search.

[69]Beneficial.

Of diet, washing, and other necessaries
Fully defrayed.

Ali. Believe it, sir, there shall no care be wanting.

Lol. Sir, an officer in this place may deserve something; the trouble will pass through my hands.

Ped. [*Giving Lollio money*] 'Tis fit something should come to your hands then, sir.

Lol. Yes, sir, 'tis I must keep him sweet,[70] and read to him; what is his name?

Ped. His name is Antonio; marry, we use but half to him, only Tony.[71]

Lol. Tony, Tony, 'tis enough, and a very good name for a fool. What's your name, Tony?

Ant. He, he, he; well, I thank you, cousin, he, he, he.

Lol. Good boy, hold up your head. He can laugh; I perceive by that he is no beast.[72]

Ped. Well, sir,
If you can raise him but to any height,
Any degree of wit, might he attain,
As I might say, to creep but on all four
Towards the chair of wit or walk on crutches,
'Twould add an honour to your worthy pains,
And a great family might pray for you,
To which he should be heir had he discretion
To claim and guide his own; assure you, sir,
He is a gentleman.

Lol. Nay, there's nobody doubted that. At first sight I knew him for a gentleman;[73] he looks no other yet.

Ped. Let him have good attendance and sweet lodging.

Lol. As good as my mistress lies in, sir, and as you allow us time and

---

[70]Clean, sweet-smelling.

[71]This name became synonymous with "fool," due in part to the popularity of *The Changeling*.

[72]Aristotle believed that man's ability to laugh distinguished him from other animals.

[73]Lollio is commenting not on his politeness, but on his social standing; he is undoubtedly poking fun at the gentry, but he may also be aware of Antonio's disguise from the start.

16

means, we can raise him to the higher degree of discretion.

Ped. Nay, there shall no cost want,[74] sir.

Lol. He will hardly be stretch'd up to the wit of a magnifico.[75]

Ped. Oh, no, that's not to be expected; far shorter will be enough.

Lol. I'll warrant you make him fit to bear office in five weeks; I'll undertake to wind him up to the wit of constable.[76]

Ped. If it be lower than that, it might serve turn.[77]

Lol. No, fie, to level him with a headborough,[78] beadle,[79] or watchman,[80] were but little better then he is; constable I'll able him:[81] if he do come to be a justice afterwards, let him thank the keeper. Or I'll go further with you; say I do bring him up to my own pitch,[82] say I make him as wise as myself.

Ped. Why, there I would have it.

Lol. Well, go to, either I'll be as arrant[83] a fool as he, or he shall be as wise as I, and then I think 'twill serve his turn.

Ped. Nay, I do like thy wit passing well.

Lol. Yes, you may; yet if I had not been a fool, I had had more wit than I have too. Remember what state you find me in.

Ped. I will, and so leave you: your best cares, I beseech you.

Ali. Take you none with you; leave 'em all with us.

Exit Pedro.

---

[74]All expenses paid.

[75]A Venetian magistrate, and by extension any high-ranking person.

[76]Often satirized for their proverbial stupidity.

[77]Be sufficient.

[78]A parish officer identical in functions with a petty constable; e.g., Verges in *Much Ado about Nothing*.

[79]A minor legal officer (warrant officer/under-bailiff), also proverbially slow-witted.

[80]A constable of the watch in charge of civil order.

[81]Make him fit for.

[82]Height.

[83]Unmitigated.

Ant. Oh, my cousin's gone; cousin, cousin, oh!

Lol. Peace, peace, Tony: you must not cry, child; you must be whipp'd if you do. Your cousin is here still; I am your cousin, Tony.

Ant. He, he, then I'll not cry, if thou beest my cousin, he, he, he.

Lol. I were best try his wit a little, that I may know what form[84] to place him in.

Ali. Ay, do, Lollio, do.

Lol. I must ask him easy questions at first. Tony, how many true fingers has a tailor on his right hand?

Ant. As many as on his left, cousin.

Lol. Good, and how many on both?

Ant. Two less than a deuce,[85] cousin.

Lol. Very well answered; I come to you again, cousin Tony: how many fools goes to a wise man?

Ant. Forty in a day sometimes, cousin.

Lol. Forty in a day? How prove you that?

Ant. All that fall out amongst themselves, and go to a lawyer to be made friends.

Lol. A parlous[86] fool; he must sit in the fourth form at least, I perceive that. I come again, Tony: how many knaves make an honest man?

Ant. I know not that, cousin.

Lol. No, the question is too hard for you: I'll tell you, cousin. There's three knaves may make an honest man, a sergeant, a jailer, and a beadle: the sergeant catches him, the jailer holds him, and the beadle lashes him; and if he be not honest then, the hangman must cure him.

Ant. Ha, ha, ha, that's fine sport, cousin.

Ali. This was too deep a question for the fool, Lollio.

---

[84]Class.

[85]Tailors were proverbially dishonest.

[86]Perilous, i.e., cunning, shrewd.

18

Lol. Yes, this might have serv'd yourself, though I say't; once more and you shall go play, Tony.

Ant. Ay, play at push-pin[87] cousin, ha, he.

Lol. So thou shalt; say how many fools are here.

Ant. Two, cousin, thou and I.

Lol. Nay, y'are too forward there, Tony; mark my question: how many fools and knaves are here? A fool before a knave, a fool behind a knave, between every two fools a knave, how many fools, how many knaves?

Ant. I never learnt so far, cousin.

Ali. Thou putt'st too hard questions to him, Lollio.

Lol. I'll make him understand it easily. Cousin, stand there.

Ant. Ay, cousin.

Lol. Master, stand you next the fool.

Ali. Well, Lollio.

Lol. Here's my place. Mark now, Tony: there a fool before a knave.

Ant. That's I, cousin.

Lol. Here's a fool behind a knave, that's I, and between us two fools there is a knave, that's my master; 'tis but we three,[88] that's all.

Ant. We three, we three, cousin.

Madmen shout from within.

1st Mad. Put's head i' th' pillory, the bread's too little!

2nd Mad. Fly, fly, and he catches the swallow![89]

3rd Mad. Give her more onion, or the devil put the rope about her crag![90]

---

[87]A child's game.

[88]Dilke notes the allusion to the sign of two idiots' heads with the legend "We three," implying that the viewer is the third.

[89]"Fly and you will catch the sparrow" was proverbial.

[90]Neck.

Lol. You may hear what time of day it is: the chimes of Bedlam[91] goes.

Ali. Peace, peace, or the wire[92] comes!

1st Mad. Cat whore, cat whore, her parmasant, her parmasant![93]

Ali. Peace, I say! Their hour's come, they must be fed, Lollio.

Lol. There's no hope of recovery of that Welsh madman: was undone by a mouse that spoil'd him a parmasant; lost his wits for't.

Ali. Go to your charge, Lollio, I'll to mine.

Lol. Go you to your madmen's ward, let me alone with your fools.

Ali. And remember my last charge, Lollio.

Lol. Of which your patients do you think I am?

[*Exit* Alibius.

Come, Tony, you must amongst your school-fellows now; there's pretty scholars amongst 'em, I can tell you: there's some of 'em at *stultus, stulta, stultum.*[94]

Ant. I would see the madmen, cousin, if they would not bite me.

Lol. No, they shall not bite thee, Tony.

Ant. They bite when they are at dinner, do they not, coz?

Lol. They bite at dinner indeed, Tony. Well, I hope to get credit by thee; I like thee the best of all the scholars that ever I brought up, and thou shalt prove a wise man, or I'll prove a fool myself.

[*Exeunt.*

---

[91]St. Mary of Bethlehem Hospital, the lunatic asylum just outside London.
[92]Whip.
[93]The madman is upbraiding his cat for not catching the mouse that ate his parmesan cheese.
[94]The Latin declension for "foolish".

ACT II.

SCENE I.

A chamber in the castle.

Enter Beatrice *and* Jasperino *severally.*[95]

Bea. Oh, sir, I'm ready now for that fair service
Which makes the name of friend sit glorious on you.
Good angels and this conduct[96] be your guide;
Fitness of time and place is there set down, sir.

[*She hands him a paper.*

Jas. The joy I shall return rewards my service.

[*Exit.*

Bea. How wise is Alsemero in his friend!
It is a sign he makes his choice with judgment.
Then I appear in nothing more approv'd
Than making choice of him;
For 'tis a principle, he that can choose
That bosom well, who of his thoughts partakes,
Proves most discreet in every choice he makes.
Methinks I love now with the eyes of judgment
And see the way to merit, clearly see it.
A true deserver like a diamond sparkles:
In darkness you may see him, that's in absence,
Which is the greatest darkness falls on love;
Yet is he best discern'd then
With intellectual eyesight. What's Piracquo
My father spends his breath for? And his blessing
Is only mine as I regard his name,
Else it goes from me, and turns head against me,
Transform'd into a curse. Some speedy way
Must be remembered; he's so forward too,
So urgent that way, scarce allows me breath
To speak to my new comforts.

[*Enter* Deflores.

---

[95]Separately, i.e., from different entrances.

[96]A pass with directions.

21

Def. [*Aside*] Yonder's she.
What ever ails me? Now alate especially
I can as well be hang'd as refrain seeing her;
Some twenty times a day, nay, not so little,
Do I force errands, frame ways and excuses
To come into her sight, and I have small reason for't,
And less encouragement; for she baits me still
Every time worse than other, does profess herself
The cruelest enemy to my face in town,
At no hand[97] can abide the sight of me,
As if danger, or ill luck, hung in my looks.
I must confess my face is bad enough,
But I know far worse has better fortune,
And not endur'd alone, but doted on;
And yet such pick-hair'd faces, chins like witches',
Here and there five hairs whispering in a corner,
As if they grew in fear one of another,
Wrinkles like troughs, where swine deformity swills
The tears of perjury that lie there like wash,[98]
Fallen from the slimy and dishonest eye.
Yet such a one plucks[99] sweets without restraint,
And has the grace of beauty to his sweet.[100]
Though my hard fate has thrust me out to servitude,
I tumbled into th' world a gentleman.
She turns her blessed eye upon me now,
And I'll endure all storms before I part with 't.

Bea. Again!
[*Aside*] This ominous ill-fac'd fellow more disturbs me
Than all my other passions!

Def. [*Aside*] Now 't begins again;
I'll stand this storm of hail though the stones pelt me.

Bea. Thy business? What's thy business?

Def. [*Aside*] Soft and fair,
I cannot part so soon now.

Bea. [*Aside*] The villain's fix'd.--

---

[97]On no account.

[98]Watery discharge.

[99]Pluckt.

[100]The blessing (i.e., that said before a meal) of her being beautiful for his desert.

22

Thou standing toad-pool!¹⁰¹

Def. [*Aside*] The shower falls amain now.

Bea. Who sent thee? What's thy errand? Leave my sight!

Def. My lord your father charg'd me to deliver
A message to you.

Bea. What, another since?
Do't and be hang'd then, let me be rid of thee!

Def. True service merits mercy.

Bea. What's thy message?

Def. Let beauty settle but in patience,
You shall hear all.

Bea. A dallying, trifling torment!

Def. Signior Alonzo de Piracquo, lady,
Sole brother to Tomazo de Piracquo--

Bea. Slave, when wilt make an end?

Def. Too soon I shall.

Bea. What all this while of him?

Def. The said Alonzo,
With the foresaid Tomazo--

Bea. Yet again!

Def. Is new alighted.

Bea. Vengeance strike the news!
Thou thing most loath'd, what cause was there in this
To bring thee to my sight?

Def. My lord your father
Charg'd me to seek you out.

Bea. Is there no other
To send his errand by?

¹⁰¹Stagnant and foul water in which the sun supposedly bred toads and other loathsome, venomous creatures.

Def. It seems 'tis my luck
To be i' th' way still.

Bea. Get thee from me.

Def. So.
[*Aside*] Why, am not I an ass to devise ways
Thus to be rail'd at? I must see her still;
I shall have a mad qualm within this hour again,
I know't, and like a common Garden bull,[102]
I do but take breath to be lugg'd[103] again.
What this may bode I know not; I'll despair the less
Because there's daily precedents of bad faces
Belov'd beyond all reason. These foul chops[104]
May come into favour one day 'mongst his fellows:
Wrangling has prov'd the mistress of good pastime;
As children cry themselves asleep, I ha' seen
Women have chid themselves abed to men.

[*Exit* Deflores.

Bea. I never see this fellow but I think
Of some harm towards me: danger's in my mind still;
I scarce leave trembling of an hour after.
The next good mood I find my father in
I'll get him quite discarded. Oh, I was
Lost in this small disturbance and forgot
Affliction's fiercer torrent that now comes,
To bear down all my comforts!

Enter Vermandero, Alonzo, Tomazo.

Ver. Y'are both welcome,
But an especial one belongs to you, sir,
To whose most noble name our love presents
The addition of a son, our son Alonzo.

Alon. The treasury of honour[105] cannot bring forth
A title I should more rejoice in, sir.

---

[102]Bull-baiting was held at the Paris Garden, an arena near the Globe Theater in Southwark.

[103]Pulled by the ear or hair, baited.

[104]Cheeks.

[105]List of honorific titles.

Ver. You have improv'd it well. Daughter, prepare;
The day will steal upon thee suddenly.

Bea. [*Aside*] Howe'er, I will be sure to keep the night,[106]
If it should come so near me.

[Vermandero *and* Beatrice *talk apart.*

Tom. Alonzo.

Alon. Brother.

Tom. In troth I see small welcome in her eye.

Alon. Fie, you are too severe a censurer[107]
Of love in all points; there's no bringing on you.[108]
If lovers should mark everything a fault,
Affection would be like an ill-set book,
Whose faults[109] might prove as big as half the volume.

Bea. That's all I do entreat.

Ver. It is but reasonable;
I'll see what my son says to't. Son Alonzo,
Here's a motion[110] made but to reprieve
A maidenhead three days longer; the request
Is not far out of reason, for indeed
The former time is pinching.

Alon. Though my joys
Be set back so much time as I could wish
They had been forward, yet since she desires it,
The time is set as pleasing as before,
I find no gladness wanting.

Ver. May I ever
Meet it in that point still. Y'are nobly welcome, sirs.

[*Exeunt* Vermandero *and* Beatrice.

Tom. So, did you mark the dullness of her parting now?

---

[106]I.e., not allow Alonzo to consummate the marriage.

[107]Judge.

[108]Persuading, with the possible overtone of sexually exciting.

[109]Printing errors.

[110]Proposal, specifically a formal legal appeal.

Alon. What dullness? Thou art so exceptious[111] still.

Tom. Why, let it go then; I am but a fool
To mark your harms so heedfully.

Alon. Where's the oversight?

Tom. Come, your faith's cozened[112] in her, strongly cozened;
Unsettle your affection with all speed
Wisdom can bring it to, your peace is ruin'd else.
Think what a torment 'tis to marry one
Whose heart is leapt into another's bosom:
If ever pleasure she receive from thee,
It comes not in thy name, or of thy gift.
She lies but with another in thine arms,
He the half-father unto all thy children
In the conception; if he get 'em not,
She helps to get 'em for him in his passions,
And how dangerous
And shameful her restraint may go in time to,
It is not to be thought on without sufferings.

Alon. You speak as if she lov'd some other then.

Tom. Do you apprehend so slowly?

Alon. Nay, and that
Be your fear only, I am safe enough;
Preserve your friendship and your counsel, brother,
For times of more distress. I should depart
An enemy, a dangerous, deadly one
To any but thyself that should but think
She knew the meaning of inconstancy,
Much less the use and practice; yet w'are friends.
Pray let no more be urg'd; I can endure
Much till I meet an injury to her,
Then I am not myself. Farewell, sweet brother;
How much w'are bound to heaven to depart lovingly!

[*Exit.*

Tom. Why, here is love's tame madness! Thus a man
Quickly steals into his vexation.

---

[111]Prone to making objections.

[112]Cheated.

SCENE II.

Another chamber.

Enter Diaphanta and Alsemero.

Dia. The place is my charge; you have kept your hour,
And the reward of a just meeting bless you.
I hear my lady coming; complete gentleman,
I dare not be too busy with my praises,
Th'are dangerous things to deal with.

Als. This goes well.
These women are the ladies' cabinets;
Things of most precious trust are lock'd into 'em.

Enter Beatrice.

Bea. I have within mine eye all my desires;
Requests that holy prayers ascend heaven for
And brings 'em down to furnish our defects
Come not more sweet to our necessities
Than thou unto my wishes.

Als. W'are so like
In our expressions, lady, that unless I borrow
The same words, I shall never find their equals.

Bea. How happy were this meeting, this embrace,
If it were free from envy! This poor kiss,
It has an enemy, a hateful one
That wishes poison to't. How well were I now
If there were none such name known as Piracquo,
Nor no such tie as the command of parents!
I should be but too much blessed.

Als. One good service
Would strike off both your fears, and I'll go near it too,
Since you are so distress'd: remove the cause,
The command ceases; so there's two fears blown out
With one and the same blast.

27

Bea. Pray let me find[113] you, sir.
What might that service be so strangely happy?

Als. The honourablest peace 'bout man, valour.
I'll send a challenge to Piracquo instantly.

Bea. How? Call you that extinguishing of fear
When 'tis the only way to keep it flaming?
Are not you ventured in the action
That's all my joys and comforts? Pray no more, sir.
Say you prevail'd, you're danger's and not mine then:
The law would claim you from me, or obscurity[114]
Be made the grave to bury you alive.
I'm glad these thoughts come forth; oh, keep not one
Of this condition, sir! Here was a course
Found to bring sorrow on her way to death:
The tears would ne'er 'a' dried till dust had chok'd 'em.
Blood-guiltiness becomes a fouler visage,
And now I think on one-- [*Aside*] I was too blame:[115]
I ha' marr'd so good a market[116] with my scorn.
'T had been done questionless. The ugliest creature
Creation fram'd for some use,[117] yet to see
I could not mark so much where it should be.

Als. Lady.

Bea. [*Aside*] Why, men of art make much of poison,
Keep one to expel another; where was my art?

Als. Lady, you hear not me.

Bea. I do especially, sir;
The present times are not so sure of our side
As those hereafter may be; we must use 'em then
As thrifty folks their wealth, sparingly now
Till the time opens.[118]

Als. You teach wisdom, lady.

---

[113]Understand.

[114]I.e., as a fugitive from the law.

[115]Blameworthy.

[116]Spoiled a good opportunity; proverbial.

[117]From the traditional doctrine that everything in nature served some purpose.

[118]Becomes more favorable.

Bea. Within there, Diaphanta!

Enter Diaphanta.

Dia. Do you call, madam?

Bea. Perfect your service, and conduct this gentleman
The private way you brought him.

Dia. I shall, madam.

Als. My love's as firm as love e'er built upon.

Exeunt Diaphanta *and* Alsemero. Enter Deflores.

Def. [*Aside*] I have watch'd this meeting, and do wonder much
What shall become of t'other; I'm sure both
Cannot be serv'd[119] unless she transgress. Happily
Then I'll put in for one: for if a woman
Fly from one point, from him she makes a husband,
She spreads and mounts then like arithmetic,
One, ten, one hundred, one thousand, ten thousand,
Proves in time sutler[120] to an army royal.
Now do I look to be most richly rail'd at,
Yet I must see her.

Bea. [*Aside*] Why, put case[121] I loath'd him
As much as youth and beauty hates a sepulcher,
Must I needs show it? Cannot I keep that secret,
And serve my turn upon him?[122] See, he's here.--
Deflores.

Def. [*Aside*] Ha, I shall run mad with joy!
She call'd me fairly by my name, Deflores,
And neither rogue nor rascal.

Bea. What ha' you done
To your face alate? Y'ave met with some good physician;
Y'ave prun'd[123] yourself, methinks: you were not wont
To look so amorously.

---

[119]With the sexual innuendo.

[120]1) a camp-follower who sells supplies to an army, 2) whore.

[121]Suppose, with a *possible* sexual pun (case = vagina).

[122]Use him for my own purposes.
[123]Preened.

Def. [*Aside*] Not I;
'Tis the same physnomy[124] to a hair and pimple
Which she call'd scurvy scarce an hour ago:
How is this?

Bea. Come hither, nearer, man.

Def. [*Aside*] I'm up to the chin in heaven!

Bea. Turn, let me see.
Fah! 'Tis but the heat of the liver,[125] I perceive 't.
I thought it had been worse.

Def. [*Aside*] Her fingers touch'd me;
She smells all amber.[126]

Bea. I'll make a water, for you shall cleanse this
Within a fortnight.

Def. With your own hands, lady?

Bea. Yes, mine own, sir; in a work of cure,
I'll trust no other.

Def. [*Aside*] 'Tis half an act of pleasure
To hear her talk thus to me.

Bea. When w'are us'd
To a hard face, 'tis not so unpleasing;
It mends still in opinion, hourly mends:
I see it by experience.

Def. [*Aside*] I was blest
To light upon this minute; I'll make use on't.

Bea. Hardness becomes the visage of a man well;
It argues service, resolution, manhood,
If cause were of employment.

Def. 'Twould be soon seen,
If e'er your ladyship had cause to use it.
I would but wish the honour of a service

---

[124]Physiognomy.

[125]Traditionally the seat of violent passions.

[126]Of ambergris, perfumed.

30

So happy as that mounts to.

Bea. [*Aside*] We shall try you.--
Oh, my Deflores!

Def. [*Aside*] How's that?
She calls me hers already, my Deflores!--
You were about to sigh out somewhat, madam.

Bea. No, was I? I forgot. Oh!

Def. There 'tis again,
The very fellow on't!

Bea. You are too quick, sir.

Def. There's no excuse for't, now I heard it twice, madam:
That sigh would fain have utterance. Take pity on't
And lend it a free word; 'las, how it labours
For liberty! I hear the murmur yet
Beat at your bosom.

Bea. Would creation--

Def. Ay, well said, that's it.

Bea. Had form'd me man.

Def. Nay, that's not it.

Bea. Oh, 'tis the soul of freedom!
I should not then be forc'd to marry one
I hate beyond all depths; I should have power
Then to oppose my loathings, nay, remove 'em
Forever from my sight.

Def. Oh, blest occasion!
[*Kneeling*] Without change to your sex, you have your wishes.
Claim so much man in me.

Bea. In thee, Deflores?
There's small cause for that.

Def. Put it not from me;
It's a service that I kneel for to you.

31

Bea. You are too violent to mean faithfully;[127]
There's horror in my service, blood and danger:
Can those be things to sue for?

Def. If you knew
How sweet it were to me to be employed
In any act of yours, you would say then
I fail'd and us'd not reverence enough
When I receive the charge on't.

Bea. [*Aside*] This is much,
Methinks; belike his wants are greedy, and
To such gold tastes like angels' food.[128]--Rise.

Def. I'll have the work first.

Bea. [*Aside*] Possible his need
Is strong upon him. [*Offering him money*] There's to encourage thee;
As thou art forward[129] and thy service dangerous,
Thy reward shall be precious.

Def. That I have thought on;
I have assur'd myself of that beforehand,
And know it will be precious: the thought ravishes!

Bea. Then take him to thy fury.

Def. I thirst for him.

Bea. Alonzo de Piracquo.

Def. [*Rises.*] His end's upon him; he shall be seen no more.

Bea. How lovely now dost thou appear to me!
Never was man dearlier rewarded.

Def. I do think of that.

Bea. Be wondrous careful in the execution.

Def. Why, are not both our lives upon the cast?[130]

---

[127]To intend honest service.

[128]Manna.

[129]Committed, courageous.

[130]Throw of the dice.

Bea. Then I throw all my fears upon thy service.

Def. They ne'er shall rise to hurt you.

Bea. When the deed's done,
I'll furnish thee with all things for thy flight;
Thou may'st live bravely in another country.

Def. Ay, ay, we'll talk of that hereafter.

Bea. [*Aside*] I shall rid myself of two inveterate loathings
At one time: Piracquo and his dog-face.

[*Exit.*

Def. Oh, my blood![131] Methinks I feel her in mine arms already,
Her wanton fingers combing out this beard,
And being pleased, praising this bad face!
Hunger and pleasure, they'll commend sometimes
Slovenly dishes and feed heartily on 'em,
Nay, which is stranger, refuse daintier for 'em.
Some women are odd feeders. I'm too loud.
Here comes the man goes supperless to bed,
Yet shall not rise tomorrow to his dinner.[132]

Enter Alonzo.

Alon. Deflores.

Def. My kind, honorable lord.

Alon. I am glad I ha' met with thee.

Def. Sir.

Alon. Thou canst show me the full strength of the castle?

Def. That I can, sir.

Alon. I much desire it.

Def. And if the ways and straits of some of the passages
Be not too tedious for you, I will assure
You worth your time and sight, my lord.

---

[131]Sexual desire.

[132]He will be killed very soon, before the evening meal.

33

Alon. Puh, that
Shall be no hinderance.

Def. I'm your servant then.
'Tis now near dinner time; 'gainst your lordship's rising[133]
I'll have the keys about me.

Alon. Thanks, kind Deflores.

Def. [*Aside*] He's safely thrust upon me beyond hopes.

[*Exeunt. In the act-time* Deflores *hides a naked rapier.*

---

[133]Before your lordship rises from the dinner table.

ACT III.

SCENE I.

A narrow passage.

Enter Alonzo *and* Deflores.

Def. Yes, here are all the keys; I was afraid, my lord,
I'd wanted for the postern:[134] this is it.
I've all, I've all, my lord: this for the sconce.[135]

Alon. 'Tis a most spacious and impregnable fort.

Def. You'll tell me more, my lord. This descent
Is somewhat narrow: we shall never pass
Well with our weapons; they'll but trouble us.

Alon. Thou sayst true.

Def. Pray let me help your lordship.

Alon. 'Tis done. Thanks, kind Deflores.

Def. Here are hooks, my lord,
To hang such things on purpose.

Alon. Lead, I'll follow thee.

> [*Exit at one door and enter at the other.*

SCENE II.

A vault.

Def. All this is nothing; you shall see anon
A place you little dream on.[136]

Alon. I am glad
I have this leisure: all your master's house
Imagine I ha' taken a gondola.

Def. All but myself, sir, [*aside*] which makes up my safety.--

---

[134]Side or back door.

[135]Small fort or earthwork.

[136]I.e., the grave.

35

My lord, I'll place you at a casement[137] here,
Will show you the full strength of all the castle.
Look, spend your eye a while upon that object.

Alon. Here's rich variety, Deflores.

Def. Yes, sir.

Alon. Goodly munition.

Def. Ay, there's ordnance,[138] sir;
No bastard metal[139] will ring you a peal like bells
At great men's funerals. Keep your eye straight, my lord;
Take special notice of that sconce before you,
There you may dwell awhile.

Alon. I am upon't.

Def. And so am I. [*Stabs him.*]

Alon. Deflores, oh, Deflores,
Whose malice hast thou put on?

Def. Do you question
A work of secrecy? I must silence you. [*Stabs him.*]

Alon. Oh, oh, oh!

Def. I must silence you. [*Stabs him; Alonzo dies.*]
So, here's an undertaking well accomplish'd.
This vault serves to good use now. Ha! What's that
Threw sparkles in my eye? Oh, 'tis a diamond
He wears upon his finger: it was well found,
This will approve the work.

[*He tries to take the ring off.*

What, so fast on?
Not part in death? I'll take a speedy course then:
Finger and all shall off. [*Cuts off his finger.*] So, now I'll clear
The passages from all suspect or fear.

[*Exit with body.*

---

[137]Window.

[138]Artillery.

[139]Impure metal.

36

SCENE III.

A room in Alibius's house.

Enter Isabella *and* Lollio.

Isa. Why, sirrah? Whence have you commission
To fetter the doors against me? If you
Keep me in a cage, pray whistle to me,
Let me be doing[140] something.

Lol. You shall be doing, if it please you; I'll whistle to you if you'll
pipe[141] after.

Isa. Is it your master's pleasure, or your own,
To keep me in this pinfold?[142]

Lol. 'Tis for my masters pleasure, lest being taken in another man's
corn, you might be pounded in another place.

Isa. 'Tis very well, and he'll prove very wise.

Lol. He says you have company enough in the house, if you please to be
sociable, of all sorts of people.

Isa. Of all sorts? Why, here's none but fools and madmen.

Lol. Very well: and where will you find any other, if you should go
abroad? There's my master, and I to boot too.

Isa. Of either sort one, a madman and a fool.

Lol. I would ev'n participate of both then if I were as you. I know y'are
half mad already; be half foolish too.

Isa. Y'are a brave, saucy rascal! Come on, sir,
Afford me then the pleasure of your bedlam;
You were commending once today to me
Your last come lunatic: what a proper[143]
Body there was without brains to guide it,
And what a pitiful delight appear'd
In that defect, as if your wisdom had found

---

[140]With the bawdy innuendo.

[141]Sing; "doing".

[142]A place for confining stray livestock.

[143]Handsome.

A mirth in madness. Pray, sir, let me partake
If there be such a pleasure.

Lol. If I do not show you the handsomest, discreetest madman, one
that I may call the understanding madman, then say I am a fool.

Isa. Well, a match, I will say so.

Lol. When you have a taste of the madman, you shall, if you please, see
Fools' College o' th' side. I seldom lock there; 'tis but shooting a bolt[144]
or two, and you are amongst 'em.

[*Exit.*

[*Within*] Come on, sir, let me see how handsomely you'll behave
yourself now.

Enter Lollio, Franciscus.

Fra. How sweetly she looks! Oh, but there's a wrinkle in her brow as
deep as philosophy. Anacreon, drink to my mistress' health; I'll pledge
it. Stay, stay, there's a spider in the cup! No, 'tis but a grape-stone:
swallow it, fear nothing, poet; so, so, lift higher.[145]

Isa. Alack, alack, 'tis too full of pity
To be laugh'd at! How fell he mad? Canst thou tell?

Lol. For love, mistress. He was a pretty poet too, and that set him
forwards first; the Muses then forsook him, he ran mad for a
chambermaid, yet she was but a dwarf neither.

Fra. Hail bright Titania![146]
Why stand'st thou idle on these flowery banks?
Oberon is dancing with his dryads.[147]
I'll gather daisies, primrose, violets,
And bind them in a verse of poesy.

Lol. [*Showing him a whip*] Not too near, you see your danger.

Fra. Oh, hold thy hand, great Diomed!

---

[144]Alluding to the proverb, "A fool's bolt is soon shot".

[145]The Greek poet Anacreon supposedly died by choking on a grape-stone while drinking wine.
Spiders were believed to be poisonous.

[146]Titania and Oberon were queen and king of the fairies.

[147]Wood nymphs.

38

Thou feed'st thy horses well,[148] they shall obey thee.
Get up;[149] Bucephalus[150] kneels. [*Gets down on all fours.*]

Lol. You see how I awe my flock? A shepherd has not his dog at more obedience.

Isa. His conscience is unquiet; sure that was
The cause of this. A proper gentleman.

Fra. Come hither, Aesculapius,[151] hide the poison.

Lol. [*Hiding his whip*] Well, 'tis hid.

Fra. [*Rising*] Didst thou never hear of one Tiresias,[152] a famous poet?

Lol. Yes, that kept tame wild-geese.[153]

Fra. That's he; I am the man.

Lol. No.

Fra. Yes, but make no words on't; I was a man seven years ago,

Lol. A stripling, I think you might.

Fra. Now I'm a woman, all feminine.

Lol. I would I might see that.

Fra. Juno struck me blind.

Lol. I'll ne'er believe that; for a woman, they say, has an eye[154] more than a man.

Fra. I say she struck me blind.

---

[148]The Thracian king Diomed feed his horses on human flesh.

[149]Mount.

[150]The horse of Alexander the Great, which only he could ride.

[151]The Greek god of medicine.

[152]The Theban soothsayer (not the poet) who was changed into a woman and then back to a man seven years; he was blinded by Juno for saying that women derived more enjoyment from sex.

[153]Prostitutes.

[154]Pudendum.

Lol. And Luna made you mad;[155] you have two trades[156] to beg with.

Fra. Luna is now big-bellied, and there's room
For both of us to ride with Hecate;[157]
I'll drag thee up into her silver sphere,
And there we'll kick the dog, and beat the bush[158]
That barks against the witches of the night.
The swift lycanthropi[159] that walks the round,
We'll tear their wolvish skins, and save the sheep. [*Beats Lollio.*]

Lol. Is't come to this? Nay, then, my poison comes forth again! Mad
slave, indeed, abuse your keeper? [*Shows him the whip.*]

Isa. I prithee hence with him, now he grows dangerous.

Fra. [*Singing*] Sweet love pity me, give me leave to lie with thee.

Lol. No, I'll see you wiser first. To your own kennel.

Fra. No noise, she sleeps, draw all the curtains round;
Let no soft sound molest the pretty soul
But love, and love creeps in at a mouse-hole.[160]

Lol. I would you would get into your hole.

[*Exit* Franciscus.

Now, mistress, I will bring you another sort; you shall be fool'd another
while. Tony, come hither, Tony, look who's yonder, Tony.

Enter Antonio.

Ant. Cousin, is it not my aunt?[161]

Lol. Yes, 'tis one of 'em, Tony.

Ant. He, he, how do you, uncle?

---

[155]Lunatics were made mad by Luna, the moon.

[156]Blindness and madness.

[157]The goddess of witchcraft and magic, also the goddess of the moon.

[158]The Man in the Moon was represented as having a lantern, a thornbush and a dog.

[159]Madmen who believe they are wolves.

[160]Pudendum.

[161]Bawd, prostitute.

Lol. Fear him not, mistress, 'tis a gentle nidget;[162] you may play with him, as safely with him as with his bauble.[163]

Isa. How long hast thou been a fool?

Ant. Ever since I came hither, cousin.

Isa. Cousin? I'm none of thy cousins, fool.[164]

Lol. Oh, mistress, fools have always so much wit as to claim their kindred.

Mad. [*within*] Bounce, bounce, he falls, he falls!

Isa. Hark you, your scholars in the upper room are out of order.

Lol. Must I come amongst you there? Keep you the fool, mistress; I'll go up and play left-handed Orlando[165] amongst the madmen.

[*Exit.*

Isa. Well, sir.

Ant. 'Tis opportuneful now, sweet lady! Nay,
Cast no amazing eye upon this change.

Isa. Ha!

Ant. This shape of folly shrouds your dearest love,
The truest servant to your powerful beauties,
Whose magic had this force thus to transform me.

Isa. You are a fine fool indeed.

Ant. Oh, 'tis not strange.
Love has an intellect that runs through all
The scrutinous sciences and, like
A cunning poet, catches a quantity
Of every knowledge, yet brings all home
Into one mystery, into one secret
That he proceeds in.

---

[162]Fool.

[163]1) the baton of the court jester, 2) penis.

[164]Isabella is offended because cousin was slang for whore.

[165]Act violently like the hero of Ariosto's *Orlando Furioso*, but "left-handedly," i.e., not too well, comically.

41

Isa. Y'are a parlous fool.

Ant. No danger in me: I bring naught but love
And his soft, wounding shafts to strike you with.
Try but one arrow;[166] if it hurt you,
I'll stand you twenty back in recompense.

Isa. A forward fool, too.

Ant. This was love's teaching;
A thousand ways he fashion'd out my way,[167]
And this I found the safest and nearest
To tread the galaxia[168] to my star.

Isa. Profound withal. Certain you dream'd of this;
Love never taught it waking.

Ant. Take no acquaintance
Of these outward follies; there is within
A gentleman that loves you.

Isa. When I see him,
I'll speak with him; so in the meantime
Keep your habit,[169] it becomes you well enough.
As you are a gentleman, I'll not discover you;
That's all the favour that you must expect.
When you are weary, you may leave the school;
For all this while you have but play'd the fool.

Enter Lollio.

Ant. And must again. He, he, I thank you, cousin;
I'll be your valentine tomorrow morning.

Lol. How do you like the fool, mistress?

Isa. Passing well, sir.

Lol. Is he not witty, pretty well for a fool?

Isa. If he hold on as he begins, he is like to come to something!

---

[166]Kiss.

[167]Taught me, prompted me.

[168]The Milky Way.

[169]Clothes.

Lol. Ay, thank a good tutor. You may put him to't; he begins to answer pretty hard questions. Tony, how many is five times six?

Ant. Five times six is six times five.

Lol. What arithmetician could have answer'd better? How many is one hundred and seven?

Ant. One hundred and seven is seven hundred and one, cousin.

Lol. This is no wit to speak on. Will you be rid of the fool now?

Isa. By no means; let him stay a little.

Mad. [*within*] Catch there, catch the last couple in hell![170]

Lol. gain? Must I come amongst you? Would my master were come home! I am not able to govern both these wards together.

[*Exit.*

Ant. Why should a minute of love's hour be lost?

Isa. Fie, out again! I had rather you kept
Your other posture: you become not your tongue
When you speak from your clothes.[171]

Ant. How can he freeze
Lives near so sweet a warmth? Shall I alone
Walk through the orchard of the Hesperides.
And cowardly not dare to pull an apple?[172]
This with the red cheeks I must venture for.

Enter Lollio *above.*

Isa. Take heed, there's giants keep 'em.

[Antonio *kisses her.*

---

[170]An allusion to the children's game barley-break, in which a couple occupy a middle ground called "hell" and try to catch two other couples as they run through it to change partners (or "break"); if caught, players remained in "hell" until the last couple remained. This exclamation has thematic implications, as we'll see later.

[171]Your speech is inconsistent with the fool's clothes you are wearing.

[172]A mythological orchard that bore golden apples, it was guarded by the Hesperides (the daughters of Atlas and Hesperus) and the hundred-headed dragon Ladon, offspring of the giant Tython.

43

Lol. How now, fool, are you good at that? Have you read Lipsius?[173]
He's past *Ars Amandi*;[174] I believe I must put harder questions to him, I
perceive that.

Isa. You are bold without fear, too.

Ant. What should I fear,
Having all joys about me? Do you smile,
And love shall play the wanton on your lip,
Meet and retire, retire and meet again:
Look you but cheerfully, and in your eyes
I shall behold mine own deformity,
And dress myself up fairer; I know this shape
Becomes me not, but in those bright mirrors
I shall array me handsomely.

Lol. [*Aside*] Cuckoo, cuckoo![175]

[*Exit.*

Enter Madmen *above, some as birds, others as beasts.*

[*Exit* Madmen.

Ant. What are these?

Isa. Of fear enough to part us,
Yet are they but our schools of lunatics,
That act their fantasies in any shapes
Suiting their present thoughts: if sad, they cry;
If mirth be their conceit, they laugh again.
Sometimes they imitate the beasts and birds,
Singing or howling, braying, barking; all
As their wild fancies prompt 'em.

Enter Lollio.

Ant. These are no fears.

Isa. But here's a large one, my man.

Ant. Ha, he, that's fine sport indeed, cousin.

---

[173]Justus Lipsius (1547-1606), a Neo-Stoic scholar; his name is mentioned merely for the pun
on "lips."

[174]Ovid's *Art of Love.*

[175]Indicating Alibius is about to be cuckolded.

44

Lol. I would my master were come home; 'tis too much for one shepherd to govern two of these flocks. Nor can I believe that one churchman can instruct two benefices at once:[176] there will be some incurable mad of the one side and very fools on the other. Come, Tony.

Ant. Prithee, cousin, let me stay here still.

Lol. No, you must to your book now you have play'd sufficiently.

Isa. Your fool is grown wondrous witty.

Lol. Well, I'll say nothing; but I do not think but he will put you down[177] one of these days.

Exeunt Lollio *and* Antonio.

Isa Here the restrained current might make breach,
Spite of the watchful bankers.[178] Would a woman stray,
She need not gad abroad to seek her sin;
It would be brought home one ways or other:
The needle's point will to the fixed north,
Such drawing arctics women's beauties are.

Enter Lollio.

Lol. How dost thou, sweet rogue?

Isa. How now?

Lol. Come, there are degrees; one fool may be better than another.

Isa. What's the matter?

Lol. Nay, if thou giv'st thy mind to fools, flesh, have at thee!

[*Tries to kiss her.*

Isa. You bold slave, you!

Lol. I could follow now as t'other fool did:
[*Imitating Antonio*] "What should I fear,
Having all joys about me? Do you smile,
And love shall play the wanton on your lip,
Meet and retire, retire and meet again:

---

[176]A reference to ecclesiastical abuses of priests holding a plurality of benefices.

[177]1) outwit you, 2) overcome you sexually.

[178]Those who repair the banks of rivers and dykes.

45

Look you but cheerfully, and in your eyes
I shall behold mine own deformity,
And dress myself up fairer; I know this shape
Becomes me not--"
And so as it follows. But is not this the more foolish way? Come, sweet
rogue, kiss me, my little Lacedemonian.[179] Let me feel how thy pulses
beat; thou hast a thing about thee would do a man pleasure, I'll lay my
hand on't.

Isa. Sirrah, no more! I see you have discovered
This love's knight-errant, who hath made adventure
For purchase of my love; be silent, mute,
Mute as a statue, or his injunction
For me enjoying shall be to cut thy throat.
I'll do it, though for no other purpose,
And be sure he'll not refuse it.

Lol. My share, that's all; I'll have my fool's part with you.

Isa. No more: your master!

Enter Alibius.

Ali. Sweet, how dost thou?

Isa. Your bounden[180] servant, sir.

Ali. Fie, fie, sweetheart,
No more of that.

Isa. You were best lock me up.

Ali. In my arms and bosom, my sweet Isabella,
I'll lock thee up most nearly. Lollio,
We have employment, we have task in hand;
At noble Vermandero's, our castle-captain,
There is a nuptial to be solemnis'd,
Beatrice Joanna his fair daughter, bride,
For which the gentleman hath bespoke[181] our pains:
A mixture of our madmen and our fools

---

[179]A Spartan, but referring specifically to the promiscuous Helen of Troy, who was captured
from there.

[180]1) bound by duty, 2) imprisoned.

[181]Commissioned.

To finish, as it were, and make the fag[182]
Of all the revels, the third night from the first.
Only an unexpected passage over,[183]
To make a frightful pleasure, that is all,
But not the all I aim at. Could we so act it,
To teach it in a wild, distracted measure,
Though out of form and figure, breaking time's head,
It were no matter: 'twould be heal'd again
In one age or other, if not in this.
This, this, Lollio: there's a good reward begun,
And will beget a bounty, be it known.

Lol. This is easy, sir, I'll warrant you. You have about you fools and
madmen that can dance very well, and 'tis no wonder your best dancers
are not the wisest men: the reason is, with often jumping they jolt their
brains down into their feet, that their wits lie more in their heels than
in their heads.

Ali. Honest Lollio, thou giv'st me a good reason
And a comfort in it.

Isa. Y'ave a fine trade on't;
Madmen and fools are a staple commodity.

Ali. Oh, wife, we must eat, wear clothes, and live:
Just at the lawyer's haven[184] we arrive,
By madmen and by fools we both do thrive.

[*Exeunt.*

SCENE IV.

A chamber in the castle.

Enter Vermandero, Alsemero, Jasperino, *and* Beatrice.

Ver. Valencia speaks so nobly of you, sir,
I wish I had a daughter now for you.

Als. The fellow of this creature were a partner
For a king's love.

---

[182]Conclusion.

[183]Brief appearance.

[184]I.e., he is exploiting the mad and the foolish just as lawyers do.

Ver. I had her fellow once, sir,
But heaven has married her to joys eternal;
'Twere sin to wish her in this vale again.
Come, sir, your friend and you shall see the pleasures
Which my health chiefly joys in.

Als. I hear the beauty of this seat largely.[185]

Ver. It falls much short of that.

[*Exeunt. Manet* Beatrice.

Bea. So, here's one step
Into my father's favour; time will fix him.
I have got him now the liberty of the house;
So wisdom by degrees works out her freedom.
And if that eye[186] be darkened that offends me--
I wait but that eclipse--this gentleman
Shall soon shine glorious in my father's liking,
Through the refulgent[187] virtue of my love.

Enter Deflores.

Def. [*Aside*] My thoughts are at a banquet for the deed:
I feel no weight in't; 'tis but light and cheap
For the sweet recompense that I set down for't.

Bea. Deflores.

Def. Lady.

Bea. Thy looks promise cheerfully.

Def. All things are answerable:[188] time, circumstance,
Your wishes and my service.

Bea. Is it done then?

Def. Piracquo is no more.

Bea. My joys start at mine eyes; our sweet'st delights

---

[185]1) enthusiastically praised, 2) everywhere I go.

[186]Alonzo's, with the scriptural allusion, "And if thine eye offend thee, pluck it out" (Matthew 18.9).

[187]Resplendent.

[188]In agreement.

48

Are evermore born weeping.

Def. I've a token[189] for you.

Bea. For me?

Def. But it was sent somewhat unwillingly:
I could not get the ring without the finger.

Bea. Bless me! What hast thou done?

Def. Why, is that more
Than killing the whole man? I cut his heart strings.
A greedy hand thrust in a dish at court
In a mistake hath had as much as this.[190]

Bea. 'Tis the first token my father made me send him.

Def. And I made him send it back again
For his last token. I was loathe to leave it,
And I'm sure dead men have no use of jewels;
He was as loath to part with't, for it stuck
As if the flesh and it were both one substance.

Bea. At the stag's fall the keeper has his fees;[191]
'Tis soon apply'd: all dead men's fees are yours, sir.
I pray bury the finger, but the stone
You may make use on shortly; the true value,
Take't of my truth, is near three hundred ducats.

Def. 'Twill hardly buy a capcase[192] for one's conscience, though,
To keep it from the worm,[193] as fine as 'tis.
Well, being my fees I'll take it;
Great men have taught me that, or else my merit
Would scorn the way on't.

Bea. It might justly, sir.
Why, thou mistak'st, Deflores: 'tis not given
In state of recompense.

---

[189]1) proof of the murder, 2) love-token.

[190]I.e., sticking a hand in the way of the carving knife and having a finger accidentally cut off.

[191]The keeper (warden of a game park) could claim as his right certain parts of a killed deer (head, skin, etc.).

[192]A case or bag for traveling.

[193]Remorse.

Def. No, I hope so, lady;
You should soon witness my contempt to't then.

Bea. Prithee, thou look'st as if thou wert offended.

Def. That were strange, lady; 'tis not possible
My service should draw such a cause from you.
Offended? Could you think so? That were much
For one of my performance, and so warm
Yet in my service.

Bea. 'Twere misery in me to give you cause, sir.

Def. I know so much; it were so, misery
In her most sharp condition.

Bea. 'Tis resolv'd then.
Look you, sir, here's three thousand golden florins;
I have not meanly thought upon thy merit.

Def. What, salary? Now you move me!

Bea. How, Deflores?

Def. Do you place me in the rank of verminous fellows
To destroy things for wages? Offer gold?
The lifeblood of man! Is anything
Valued too precious for my recompense?

Bea. I understand thee not.

Def. I could ha' hir'd
A journeyman[194] in murder at this rate,
And mine own conscience might have slept at ease
And have had the work brought home!

Bea. [*Aside*] I'm in a labyrinth;
What will content him? I would fain be rid of him.--
I'll double the sum, sir.

Def. You take a course
To double my vexation, that's the good you do.

Bea. [*Aside*] Bless me! I am now in worse plight than I was;
I know not what will please him.--For my fear's sake,

---

[194]A professional laborer; here, a hired assassin.

I prithee make away with all speed possible.
And if thou be'st so modest not to name
The sum that will content thee, paper blushes not:
Send thy demand in writing, it shall follow thee;
But prithee take thy flight.

Def. You must fly too then.

Bea. I?

Def. I'll not stir a foot else.

Bea. What's your meaning?

Def. Why, are not you as guilty, in, I'm sure,
As deep as I? And we should stick together.
Come, your fears counsel you but ill: my absence
Would draw suspect upon you instantly;
There were no rescue for you.

Bea. [*Aside*] He speaks home.

Def. Nor is it fit we two engag'd so jointly
Should part and live asunder.

[*He tries to kiss her.*

Bea. How now, sir?
This shows not well.

Def. What makes your lip so strange?
This must not be 'twixt us.

Bea. [*Aside*] The man talks wildly.

Def. Come, kiss me with a zeal now!

Bea. [*Aside*] Heaven, I doubt[195] him!

Def. I will not stand so long to beg 'em shortly.

Bea. Take heed, Deflores, of forgetfulness;
'Twill soon betray us.

Def. Take you heed first;
Faith, y'are grown much forgetful: y'are too blame in't.

---

[195]Fear.

51

Bea. [*Aside*] He's bold, and I am blam'd for't.

Def. I have eas'd
You of your trouble; think on't: I'm in pain
And must be eas'd of you; 'tis a charity.
Justice invites your blood to understand me.

Bea. I dare not.

Def. Quickly.

Bea. Oh, I never shall!
Speak it yet further off that I may lose
What has been spoken, and no sound remain on't!
I would not hear so much offence again
For such another deed.

Def. Soft, lady, soft;
The last is not yet paid for. Oh, this act
Has put me into spirit;[196] I was as greedy on't
As the parch'd earth of moisture when the clouds weep.
Did you not mark I wrought myself into't?[197]
Nay, sued and kneel'd for't? Why was all that pains took?
You see I have thrown contempt upon your gold;
Not that I want it not, for I do piteously:
In order I will come unto't and make use on't.
But 'twas not held so precious to begin with,
For I place wealth after the heels of pleasure,
And were I not resolv'd in my belief
That thy virginity were perfect in thee,
I should but take my recompense with grudging,
As if I had but half my hopes I agreed for.

Bea. Why, 'tis impossible thou canst be so wicked,
Or shelter such a cunning cruelty,
To make his death the murderer of my honour!
Thy language is so bold and vicious,
I cannot see which way I can forgive it
With any modesty.

Def. Push, you forget yourself:
A woman dipp'd in blood and talk of modesty!

---

[196] 1) courage, 2) sexual desire.

[197] Worked to be given the task.

Bea. Oh, misery of sin! Would I had been bound
Perpetually unto my living hate
In that Piracquo than to hear these words!
Think but upon the distance that creation
Set 'twixt thy blood and mine,[198] and keep thee there.

Def. Look but into your conscience, read me there:
'Tis a true book; you'll find me there your equal.
Push, fly not to your birth, but settle you
In what the act has made you; y'are no more[199] now.
You must forget your parentage to me;
Y'are the deeds creature: by that name
You lost your first condition,[200] and I challenge you,
As peace and innocency has turn'd you out
And made you one with me.

Bea. With thee, foul villain?

Def. Yes, my fair murderess. Do you urge me?
Though thou writ'st maid, thou whore in thy affection,
'Twas chang'd from thy first love, and that's a kind
Of whoredom in thy heart; and he's chang'd now
To bring thy second on, thy Alsemero,
Whom, by all sweets that ever darkness tasted,
If I enjoy thee not, thou ne'er enjoy'st.
I'll blast the hopes and joys of marriage;
I'll confess all, my life I rate at nothing.

Bea. Deflores.

Def. I shall rest from all lovers' plagues then;
I live in pain now: that shooting eye
Will burn my heart to cinders.

Bea. Oh, sir, hear me!

Def. She that in life and love refuses me,
In death and shame my partner she shall be.

Bea. Stay, hear me once for all: I make thee master
Of all the wealth I have in gold and jewels;
Let me go poor unto my bed with honour

---

[198]I.e., the difference in their social ranks.

[199]I.e., no more than a murderess.

[200]Original innocence.

And I am rich in all things.

Def. Let this silence thee:
The wealth of all Valencia shall not buy
My pleasure from me.
Can you weep fate from its determin'd purpose?
So soon may you weep me.

Bea. Vengeance begins;
Murder, I see, is followed by more sins.
Was my creation in the womb so curs'd
It must engender with a viper first?[201]

Def. Come, rise and shroud your blushes in my bosom;
Silence is one of pleasure's best receipts:[202]
Thy peace is wrought forever in this yielding.
'Las, how the turtle[203] pants! Thou'lt love anon
What thou so fear'st and faint'st to venture on.

[*Exeunt.*

Dumb Show.

Enter Gentlemen, Vermandero *meeting them with action of wonderment
at the flight of* Alonzo de Piracquo. *Enter* Alsemero *with* Jasperino *and
Gallants;* Vermandero *points to him, the* Gentlemen *seeming to applaud
the choice.* [*Exeunt* Vermandero,] Alsemero, Jasperino, and Gentlemen
and Gallants. *Enter* Beatrice *the bride, following in great state,
accompanied with* Diaphanta, Isabella, *and other* Gentlewomen. Enter
Deflores *after all, smiling at the accident;* Alonzo's Ghost *appears to*
Deflores *in the midst of his smile, startles him, showing him the hand
whose finger he had cut off. They pass over in great solemnity.*

---

[201]"Was a curse laid on me in my mother's womb, condemning me to make love with a hideous, unnatural being before I could do so with a normal man?" (Frost), more of the Fall of Man imagery predominant in this section.

[202]Recipes.

[203]Turtledove.

54

ACT IV.

SCENE I.

Alsemero's chamber.

Enter Beatrice.

Bea. This fellow has undone me endlessly;[204]
Never was bride so fearfully distress'd.
The more I think upon th' ensuing night,
And whom I am to cope with in embraces--
One who's ennobled both in blood and mind,
So clear in understanding, that's my plague now,
Before whose judgment will my fault appear
Like malefactors' crimes before tribunals,
There is no hiding on't--the more I dive
Into my own distress. How a wise man
Stands for a great calamity! There's no venturing
Into his bed, what course soe'er I light upon,
Without my shame, which may grow up to danger.
He cannot but in justice strangle me
As I lie by him, as a cheater use me;
'Tis a precious craft to play with a false die
Before a cunning gamester.[205] Here's his closet,
The key left in't, and he abroad i' th' park.
Sure 'twas forgot; I'll be so bold as look in't.
Bless me! A right physician's closet 'tis,
Set round with vials, every one her mark too.
Sure he does practice physic for his own use,
Which may be safely call'd your great man's wisdom.[206]
What manuscript lies here? *The Book of Experiment,*
Call'd Secrets in Nature:[207] so 'tis, 'tis so.
[*Reading*] "How to know whether a woman be with child or no."
I hope I am not yet; if he should try, though--
Let me see, folio forty-five. Here 'tis,
The leaf tuck'd down upon't, the place suspicious.
[*Reading*] "If you would know whether a woman be with child or not,

---

[204]1) ravished me again and again, 2) condemned my soul eternally.

[205]Gambler and/or lecher.

[206]I.e., because it protects great men from being poisoned.

[207]*De Arcanis Naturae* by Antonius Mizaldus (1520-78) does not mention the following experiments; similar experiments appear in his *Centuriae IX. Memorabilium.*

55

give her two spoonfuls of the white water in glass C."
Where's that glass C? Oh, yonder I see't now.
[*Reading*] "And if she be with child, she sleeps full twelve hours after; if not, not."
None of that water comes into my belly.
I'll know you from a hundred; I could break you now
Or turn you into milk, and so beguile
The master of the mystery, but I'll look to[208] you.
Ha! That which is next, is ten times worse.
[*Reading*] "How to know whether a woman be a maid or not."
If that should be apply'd, what would become of me?
Belike he has a strong faith of my purity,
That never yet made proof; but this he calls
[*Reading*] "A merry slight[209] but true experiment,
The author, Antonius Mizaldus.
Give the party you suspect the quantity of a spoonful of the water in the glass M, which upon her that is a maid makes three several[210] effects: 'twill make her incontinently[211] gape, then fall into a sudden sneezing, last into a violent laughing; else dull, heavy, and lumpish."
Where had I been?
I fear it, yet 'tis seven hours to bedtime.

Enter Diaphanta.

Dia. Cuds,[212] madam, are you here?

Bea. [*Aside*] Seeing that wench now,
A trick comes in my mind; 'tis a nice piece[213]
Gold cannot purchase.--I come hither, wench,
To look my lord.

Dia. [*Aside*] Would I had such a cause
To look him too.--Why, he's i' th' park, madam.

Bea. There let him be.

Dia. Ay, madam, let him compass

---

[208]Watch out for.

[209]Trifle, or sleight.

[210]Distinct.

[211]Immediately and uncontrollably.

[212]A corruption of "God;" for this oath and variations.

[213]Scrupulous girl.

Whole parks and forests, as great rangers do;
At roosting time a little lodge can hold 'em.
Earth-conquering Alexander,[214] that thought the world
Too narrow for him, in the end had but his pit-hole.[215]

Bea. I fear thou art not modest, Diaphanta.

Dia. Your thoughts are so unwilling to be known, madam;
'Tis ever the bride's fashion towards bedtime
To set light by her joys, as if she ow'd[216] 'em not.

Bea. Her joys? Her fears, thou wouldst say.

Dia. Fear of what?

Bea. Art thou a maid, and talk'st so to a maid?
You leave a blushing business behind,
Beshrew your heart for't.

Dia. Do you mean good sooth, madam?

Bea. Well, if I'd thought upon the fear at first,
Man should have been unknown.

Dia. Is't possible?

Bea. I will give a thousand ducats to that woman
Would try what my fear were, and tell me true
Tomorrow when she gets from 't: as she likes
I might perhaps be drawn to 't.

Dia. Are you in earnest?

Bea. Do you get the woman, then challenge me,
And see if I'll fly from 't; but I must tell you
This by the way, she must be a true maid,
Else there's no trial, my fears are not hers else.

Dia. Nay, she that I would put into your hands, madam,

---

[214]Alexander the Great; cf. Juvenal's *Satire X* 168-72.

[215]Daalder, whose edition best highlights the sexual innuendo in this play, explains Diaphanta's response: "*Pit-hole* means 'grave', but there is also a definite bawdy innuendo in this context.., so Beatrice's reaction is logical. Further bawdy possibilities are *parks* = female bodies, *rangers* [gamekeepers, but also rakes, those who range for sexual conquest] = penises, *lodge* = vagina, *end* = vagina...but the effect is more subtle if the only clear pun is at the end with ["roosting time"] providing a hint."

[216]Owned.

Shall be a maid.

Bea. You know I should be sham'd else,
Because she lies[217] for me.

Dia. 'Tis a strange humour:[218]
But are you serious still? Would you resign
Your first night's pleasure and give money too?

Bea. As willingly as live. [*Aside*] Alas, the gold
Is but a by-bet to wedge in the honour.[219]

Dia. I do not know how the world goes abroad
For faith or honesty; there's both requir'd in this.
Madam, what say you to me, and stray no further?
I've a good mind, in troth, to earn your money.

Bea. Y'are too quick, I fear, to be a maid.

Dia. How? Not a maid? Nay, then, you urge me, madam,
Your honourable self is not a truer
With all your fears upon you--

Bea. [*Aside*] Bad enough then.

Dia. Then I with all my lightsome joys about me.

Bea. I'm glad to hear 't; then you dare put your honesty
Upon an easy trial.

Dia. Easy? Anything.

Bea. [*Going to the closet*] I'll come to you straight.

Dia. [*Aside*] She will not search me, will she,
Like the forewoman of a female jury?[220]

Bea. Glass M. Ay, this is it. Look, Diaphanta,
You take no worse than I do.

[*She drinks and hands* Diaphanta *the glass.*

---

[217]1) deceives, 2) lies in bed.

[218]Whim.

[219]Side-bet to get her to stake her honor.

[220]An allusion to the divorce trial of the Countess of Essex in 1613, who alleged that her marriage had not been consummated and was examined by a group of matrons; cf. the second chapter of Bromham and Bruzzi's The Changeling *and the Years of Crisis.*

Dia. And in so doing
I will not question what 'tis, but take it.

[*She drinks.*

Bea. [*Aside*] Now if the experiment be true, 'twill praise itself,
And give me noble ease. [*Diaphanta gapes.*] Begins already,
There's the first symptom. [*Diaphanta sneezes.*] And what haste it makes

To fall into the second, there by this time:
Most admirable secret! On the contrary,
It stirs not me a whit, which most concerns it.

Dia. Ha, ha, ha!

Bea. [*Aside*] Just in all things and in order,
As if 'twere circumscrib'd,[221] one accident[222]
Gives way unto another.

Dia. Ha, ha, ha!

Bea. How now, wench?

Dia. Ha, ha, ha, I am so, so light
At heart, ha, ha, ha. so pleasurable!
But one swig more, sweet madam.

Bea. Ay, tomorrow;
We shall have time to sit by 't.

Dia. Now I'm sad again.

Bea. [*Aside*] It lays itself[223] so gently too.--Come, wench,
Most honest Diaphanta I dare call thee now.

Dia. Pray tell me, madam, what trick call you this?

Bea. I'll tell thee all hereafter; we must study
The carriage of this business.

Dia. I shall carry 't well
Because I love the burthen.

---

[221]Written down for her to follow.

[222]Symptom.

[223]Subsides.

Bea. About midnight
You must not fail to steal forth gently
That I may use the place.

Dia. Oh, fear not, madam;
I shall be cool by that time. The bride's place,
And with a thousand ducats! I'm for a justice now:
I bring a portion[224] with me; I scorn small fools!

[*Exeunt.*

SCENE II.

A chamber in the castle.

Enter Vermandero *and* Servant.

Ver. I tell thee, knave, mine honour is in question,
A thing till now free from suspicion,
Nor ever was there cause. Who of my gentlemen are absent?
Tell me and truly how many and who.

Serv. Antonio, sir, and Franciscus.

Ver. When did they leave the castle?

Serv. Some ten days since, sir, the one intending to Briamata,[225] th'other
for Valencia.

Ver. The time accuses 'um: a charge of murder
Is brought within my castle gate, Piracquo's murder;
I dare not answer faithfully their absence.
A strict command of apprehension
Shall pursue 'um suddenly, and either wipe
The stain off clear or openly discover it.
Provide me winged warrants for the purpose.

Enter Tomazo.

See, I am set on again.

[*Exit* Servant.

Tom. I claim a brother of you.

---

[224]Dowry.

[225]The location of Vermandero's house in the Reynolds source.

60

Ver. Y'are too hot;
Seek him not here.

Tom. Yes, 'mongst your dearest bloods;
If my peace find no fairer satisfaction,
This is the place must yield account for him,
For here I left him, and the hasty tie
Of this snatch'd marriage gives strong testimony
Of his most certain ruin.

Ver. Certain falsehood!
This is the place indeed; his breach of faith
Has too much marr'd both my abused love,
The honourable love I reserv'd for him,
And mock'd my daughter's joy. The prepar'd morning
Blush'd at his infidelity; he left
Contempt and scorn to throw upon those friends
Whose belief hurt 'em: oh, 'twas most ignoble
To take his flight so unexpectedly
And throw such public wrongs on those that lov'd him!

Tom. Then this is all your answer?

Ver. 'Tis too fair
For one of his alliance,[226] and I warn you
That this place no more see you.

[*Exit.*

Enter Deflores.

Tom. The best is,
There is more ground to meet a man's revenge on.
Honest Deflores.

Def. That's my name indeed.
Saw you the bride? Good sweet sir, which way took she?

Tom. I have blest mine eyes from seeing such a false one.

Def. [*Aside*] I'd fain get off; this man's not for my company:
I smell his brother's blood when I come near him.

Tom. Come hither, kind and true one; I remember
My brother lov'd thee well.

---

[226]Family.

61

Def. Oh, purely, dear sir!
[*Aside*] Methinks I am now again a-killing on him,
He brings it so fresh to me.

Tom. Thou canst guess, sirrah,
One honest friend has an instinct of jealousy
At some foul guilty person.

Def. 'Las, sir,
I am so charitable, I think none
Worse than myself. You did not see the bride then?

Tom. I prithee name her not. Is she not wicked?

Def. No, no, a pretty, easy, round-pack'd sinner,[227]
As your most ladies are, else you might think
I flatter'd her; but, sir, at no hand wicked
Till th'are so old their sins and vices meet,
And they salute witches. I am call'd, I think, sir.
[*Aside*] His company ev'n o'erlays[228] my conscience.

[*Exit.*

Tom. That Deflores has a wondrous honest heart.
He'll bring it out in time, I'm assur'd on't.

Enter Alsemero.

[*Aside*] Oh, here's the glorious master of the day's joy.
'Twill not be long till he and I do reckon.--Sir.

Als. You are most welcome.

Tom. You may call that word back;
I do not think I am, nor wish to be.

Als. 'Tis strange you found the way to this house then.

Tom. Would I'd ne'er known the cause. I'm none of those, sir,
That come to give you joy and swill your wine;
'Tis a more precious liquor that must lay[229]
The fiery thirst I bring.

---

[227]A vessel of insignificant sins in a curvaceous form.

[228]Oppresses.

[229]Allay.

Als. Your words and you
Appear to me great strangers.

Tom. Time and our swords
May make us more acquainted; this the business:
I should have a brother in your place;
How treachery and malice have dispos'd of him,
I'm bound to enquire of him which holds his right,
Which never could come fairly.

Als. You must look
To answer for that word, sir.

Tom. Fear you not;
I'll have it ready drawn[230] at our next meeting.
Keep your day solemn. Farewell, I disturb it not;
I'll bear the smart with patience for a time.

[*Exit.*

Als. 'Tis somewhat ominous, this, a quarrel entered
Upon this day; my innocence relieves me,
I should be wondrous sad else.

Enter Jasperino.

Jasperino, I have news to tell thee, strange news.

Jas. I ha' some too,
I think as strange as yours; would I might keep
Mine, so my faith and friendship might be kept in't.
Faith, sir, dispense a little with my zeal,
And let it cool in this.

Als. This puts me on,[231]
And blames thee for thy slowness.

Jas. All may prove nothing,
Only a friendly fear that leapt from me, sir.

Als. No question it may prove nothing; let's partake it, though.

Jas. 'Twas Diaphanta's chance--for to that wench

---

[230]His sword, with the continued imagery of legal documents.

[231]Makes me curious.

63

I pretend[232] honest love, and she deserves it--
To leave me in a back part of the house,
A place we chose for private conference;
She was no sooner gone, but instantly
I heard your bride's voice in the next room to me
And, lending more attention, found Deflores
Louder then she.

Als. Deflores? Thou art out[233] now.

Jas. You'll tell me more anon.

Als. Still I'll prevent thee:
The very sight of him is poison to her.

Jas. That made me stagger too, but Diaphanta
At her return confirm'd it.

Als. Diaphanta!

Jas. Then fell we both to listen, and words pass'd
Like those that challenge interest in a woman.

Als. Peace, quench thy zeal; 'tis dangerous to thy bosom

Jas. Then truth is full of peril.

Als. Such truths are.
Oh, were she the sole glory of the earth,
Had eyes that could shoot fire into kings' breasts,
And touch'd,[234] she sleeps not here; yet I have time,
Though night be near, to be resolv'd hereof,
And prithee do not weigh me by my passions.

Jas. I never weigh'd friend so.

Als. Done charitably.
[*Giving him a key*] That key will lead thee to a pretty secret
By a Chaldean[235] taught me, and I've made
My study upon some; bring from my closet

---

[232]Proffer.

[233]Mistaken.

[234]

[235]An astrologer; the term derives from the Chaldeans, a tribe of wizards in the Bible (Daniel 2.2).

A glass inscrib'd there with the letter M,
And question not my purpose.

Jas. It shall be done, sir.

[Exit.

Als. How can this hang together? Not an hour since
Her woman came pleading her lady's fears,
Deliver'd her for the most timorous virgin
That ever shrunk at man's name, and so modest
She charg'd her weep out her request to me
That she might come obscurely[236] to my bosom.

Enter Beatrice.

Bea. [*Aside*] All things go well; my woman's preparing yonder
For her sweet voyage, which grieves me to lose:
Necessity compels it; I lose all else.

Als. [*Aside*] Push, modesty's shrine is set in yonder forehead.
I cannot be too sure though.--My Joanna.

Bea. Sir, I was bold to weep a message to you;
Pardon my modest fears.

Als. [*Aside*] The dove's not meeker.
She's abus'd, questionless.

Enter Jasperino.

Oh, are you come, sir?

Bea. [*Aside*] The glass, upon my life! I see the letter.

Jas. Sir, this is M.

Als. 'Tis it.

Bea. [*Aside*] I am suspected.

Als. How fitly our bride comes to partake with us!

Bea. What is't, my lord?

Als. No hurt.

---

[236]In darkness.

Bea. Sir, pardon me,
I seldom taste of any composition.[237]

Als. But this upon my warrant you shall venture on.

Bea. I fear 'twill make me ill.

Als. Heaven forbid that.

Bea. [*Aside*] I'm put now to my cunning; th' effects I know,
If I can now but feign 'em handsomely.

Als. [*Aside to Jasperino*] It has that secret virtue it ne'er miss'd, sir,
Upon a virgin.

Jas. [*Aside to Alsemero*] Treble qualitied.

[Beatrice *gapes, then sneezes.*

Als. [*Aside to Jasperino*] By all that's virtuous, it takes there, proceeds!

Jas. [*Aside to Alsemero*] This is the strangest trick to know a maid by.

Bea. Ha, ha, ha!
You have given me joy of heart to drink, my lord.

Als. No, thou hast given me such joy of heart
That never can be blasted.

Bea. What's the matter, sir?

Als. [*Aside to Jasperino*] See, now 'tis settled in a melancholy,
Keeps both the time and method.--My Joanna,
Chaste as the breath of heaven or morning's womb
That brings the day forth, thus my love encloses thee.

[*He embraces her.*

[*Exeunt.*

SCENE III.

A room in Alibius's house.

Enter Isabella *and* Lollio.

Isa. Oh heaven! Is this the waiting moon?

---

[237]Mixture.

Does love turn fool, run mad, and all at once?
Sirrah, here's a madman akin to the fool too,
A lunatic lover.

Lol. No, no, not he I brought the letter from.

Isa. Compare his inside with his out[238] and tell me.

Lol. The out's mad, I'm sure of that; I had a taste on't. [*Reading*] "To
the bright Andromeda, chief chambermaid to the knight of the sun, at
the sign of Scorpio, in the middle region, sent by the bellows-mender
of Æolus. Pay the post." This is stark madness.

Isa. Now mark the inside. [*He opens the letter and she reads over his
shoulder.*] "Sweet lady, having now cast off this counterfeit cover of a
madman, I appear to your best judgment a true and faithful lover of
your beauty."

Lol. He is mad still.

Isa. [*Reading*] "If any fault you find, chide those perfections in you
which have made me imperfect; 'tis the same sun that causeth to grow
and enforceth to wither"--

Lol. Oh, rogue!

Isa. [*Reading*] "Shapes and transhapes, destroys and builds again. I
come in winter to you dismantled[239] of my proper ornaments; by the
sweet splendour of your cheerful smiles, I spring and live a lover."

Lol. Mad rascal still.

Isa. [*Reading*] "Tread him not under foot that shall appear an honour to
your bounties. I remain, mad till I speak with you, from whom I expect
my cure, yours all, or one beside himself, Franciscus."

Lol. You are like to have a fine time on't. My master and I may give
over our professions; I do not think but you can cure fools and
madmen faster than we, with little pains too.

Isa. Very likely.

Lol. One thing I must tell you, mistress: you perceive that I am privy to

---

[238]1) the true letter with the message on its cover, 2) Franciscus's true intent with his disguise.
[239]Stripped.

67

your skill; if I find you minister once and set up the trade,[240] I put in for my thirds.[241] I shall be mad or fool else.

Isa. The first place is thine, believe it, Lollio;
If I do fall--

Lol. I fall upon you.

Isa. So.

Lol. Well, I stand to[242] my venture.

Isa. But thy counsel now: how shall I deal with 'um?

Lol. Why, do you mean to deal with[243] 'um?

Isa. Nay, the fair understanding:[244] how to use 'um.

Lol. Abuse 'um: that's the way to mad the fool and make a fool of the madman, and then you use 'um kindly.[245]

Isa. 'Tis easy. I'll practise;[246] do thou observe it:
The key of thy wardrobe.

                              [*He gives her the key.*

Lol. There; fit yourself for 'um, and I'll fit 'um both for you.

Isa. Take thou no further notice than the outside.

                                                    [*Exit.*

Lol. Not an inch; I'll put you to the inside.[247]

                    Enter Alibius.

Ali. Lollio, art there? Will all be perfect, think'st thou?
Tomorrow night, as if to close up the solemnity,

---

[240]Commit adultery and become a whore.

[241]A third share, the portion of an estate inherited by the widow, with the sexual implication.
[242]Abide by.

[243]Cope, with the sexual innuendo.

[244]Decent interpretation.

[245]1) gently, 2) according to the natures.

[246]Scheme.

[247]Put to = have intercourse.

Vermandero expects us.

Lol. I mistrust the madmen most; the fools will do well enough:
I have taken pains with them.

Ali. Tush, they cannot miss; the more absurdity,
The more commends it, so no rough behaviours
Affright the ladies: they are nice things, thou know'st.

Lol. You need not fear, sir; so long as we are there with our
commanding pizzles,[248] they'll be as tame as the ladies themselves.

Ali. I will see them once more rehearse before they go.

Lol. I was about it, sir; look you to the madmen's morris,[249] and let me
alone with the other. There is one or two that I mistrust their fooling;
I'll instruct them, and then they shall rehearse the whole measure.

Ali. Do so; I'll see the music prepar'd: but, Lollio,
By the way, how does my wife brook her restraint?
Does she not grudge at it?

Lol. So, so. She takes some pleasure in the house; she would abroad
else. You must allow her a little more length; she's kept too short.

Ali. She shall along to Vermandero's with us;
That will serve her for a month's liberty.

Lol. What's that on your face, sir?

Ali. Where, Lollio? I see nothing.

Lol. Cry you mercy, sir, 'tis your nose! It show'd like the trunk of a
young elephant.[250]

Ali. Away, rascal: I'll prepare the music, Lollio.

Exit Alibius.

Lol. Do, sir; and I'll dance the whilst. Tony, where art thou, Tony?

Enter Antonio.

Ant. Here, cousin. Where art thou?

---

[248]Whips made from the dried penises of bulls.

[249]Country dance.

[250]Perhaps indicating that Alibius is being led by the nose.

Lol. Come, Tony, the footmanship I taught you.

Ant. I had rather ride,[251] cousin.

Lol. Ay, a whip take you, but I'll keep you out. Vault in; look you, Tony: [*dancing*] fa, la la la la.

Ant. [*Dancing*] Fa, la la la la.

Lol. There, an honour.[252]

Ant. Is this an honour, coz? [*Bows.*]

Lol. Yes, and it please your worship.

Ant. Does honour bend in the hams,[253] coz?

Lol. Marry, does it, as low as worship, squireship, nay, yeomanry itself sometimes, from whence it first stiffened. There rise a caper.[254]

Ant. Caper after an honour, coz?

Lol. Very proper, for honour is but a caper, rises as fast and high, has a knee or two, and falls to th' ground again. You can remember your figure,[255] Tony?

[*Exit.*

Ant. Yes, cousin, when I see thy figure, I can remember mine.

Enter Isabella *dressed as a madwoman.* Antonio *resumes dancing.*

Isa. Hey, how he treads the air!
Shoo, shoo, t'other way: he burns his wings else;
Here's wax enough below, Icarus,[256] more
Than will be canceled[257] these eighteen moons.

---

[251]With the sexual innuendo.

[252]A bow.

[253]This is ostensibly an inquiry about the right execution of the bow, but with the punning query, 'Do those of high rank abase themselves so?'

[254]An upward leap.

[255]1) dance steps, 2) appearance.

[256]Isabella's following "madness" links Antonio to Icarus, the son of the architect Daedalus, who built them wings from wax and feathers, but who flew too close to the sun and plunged into the sea after the wax melted. In one version, they were escaping the labyrinth that Daedalus had built, the labyrinth that held the Minotaur.

[257]Terminology alluding to the sealing wax on legal documents, possibly her marriage contracts.

70

He's down, he's down; what a terrible fall he had!
Stand up, thou son of Cretan Dedalus,
And let us tread the lower labyrinth;[258]
I'll bring thee to the clue.[259]

Ant. Prithee, coz, let me alone.

Isa. Art thou not drown'd?
About thy head I saw a heap of clouds
Wrapp'd like a Turkish turban on thy back,
A crook'd chameleon-colour'd rainbow hung
Like a tiara down unto thy hams.
Let me suck out those billows in thy belly;[260]
Hark how they roar and rumble in the straits![261]
Bless thee from the pirates.

                                        [*Attempts to kiss him.*

Ant. Pox upon you, let me alone!

Isa. Why shouldst thou mount so high as Mercury[262]
Unless thou hadst reversion[263] of his place?
Stay in the moon with me, Endymion,[264]
And we will rule these wild rebellious waves
That would have drown'd my love.

Ant. I'll kick thee if again thou touch me,
Thou wild unshapen antic;[265] I am no fool,
You bedlam!

---

[258]With the sexual innuendo.

[259]An allusion to the ball of thread (pun on "clew") that Ariadne gave to Theseus, which allowed him to find his way out of the labyrinth after killing the Minotaur.

[260]A turban with a long tailpiece.

[261]1) the Icarian Sea between Crete and Greece, 2) intestines (Isabella has her ear to Antonio's midsection).

[262]Winged messenger and herald of the gods.

[263]The right of succession.

[264]The handsome shepherd youth loved by Luna, whom Isabella imagines herself to be, controlling the tides. Isabella's method of rapidly changing the classical identities she gives Antonio and herself is significant. First, she is parodying Antonio and Franciscus, who themselves in their disguises of fool and madman are parodies (or devaluations) of the classical standards of the Renaissance (standards of love, beauty, bravery, etc.). Second, this rapid shifting of identities reinforces those themes to which the play's title alludes.

[265]Clown, grotesque figure.

Isa. But you are as sure as I am, mad.
Have I put on this habit of a frantic[266]
With love as full of fury to beguile
The nimble eye of watchful jealousy,
And am I thus rewarded?

Ant. Ha, dearest beauty!

Isa. No, I have no beauty now,
Nor never had, but what was in my garments.
You a quick-sighted lover? Come not near me.
Keep your caparisons,[267] y'are aptly clad;
I came a feigner to return stark mad.

[Exit.

Enter Lollio.

Ant. Stay, or I shall change condition
And become as you are.

Lol. Why, Tony, whither now? Why, fool!

Ant. Whose fool, usher of idiots? You coxcomb!
I have fool'd too much.

Lol. You were best be mad another while then.

Ant. So I am, stark mad, I have cause enough;
And I could throw the full effects on thee,
And beat thee like a fury.

Lol. Do not, do not! I shall not forbear the gentleman under the fool, if
you do. Alas, I saw through your fox-skin[268] before now. Come, I can
give you comfort: my mistress loves you, and there is as arrant a
madman i' th' house as you are a fool, your rival, whom she loves not.
If after the masque we can rid her of him, you earn her love, she says,
and the fool shall ride her.

Ant. May I believe thee?

Lol. Yes, or you may choose whether you will or no.

---

[266]Lunatic.

[267]The coverings of a horse, and by extension, clothes.

[268]Disguise.

72

Ant. She's eas'd of him; I have a good quarrel on't.

Lol. Well, keep your old station yet, and be quiet.

Ant. Tell her I will deserve her love.

Lol. And you are like to have your desire.

[*Exit Antonio.*

Enter Franciscus.

Fra. Down, down, down a-down a-down, and then with a horse-trick[269]
To kick Latona's forehead and break her bow string.[270]

Lol. [*Aside*] This is t'other counterfeit; I'll put him out of his humour.
[*Reading*] "Sweet lady, having now cast this counterfeit cover of a
madman, I appear to your best judgment a true and faithful lover of
your beauty." This is pretty well for a madman.

Fra. Ha! What's that?

Lol. [*Reading*] "Chide those perfections in you which made me
imperfect."

Fra. I am discover'd to the fool.

Lol. [*Aside*] I hope to discover the fool in you ere I have done with you.
[*Reading*] "Yours all, or one beside himself, Franciscus." [*Aside*] This
madman will mend sure.

Fra. What do you read, sirrah?

Lol. Your destiny, sir; you'll be hang'd for this trick and another that I
know.

Fra. Art thou of counsel with thy mistress?

Lol. Next her apron strings.

Fra. Give me thy hand.

Lol. Stay, let me put yours[271] in my pocket first. [*Puts the letter in his*

---

[269]A horse-like leap, possibly with a pun on "whore's trick".

[270]Latona is the Latin form of Leto, the mother of Artemis/Diana the huntress; Franciscus has
confused the two.

[271]Your letter.

pocket.] Your hand is true, is it not? It will not pick?[272] I partly fear it, because I think it does lie.

Fra. Not in a syllable.

Lol. So, if you love my mistress so well as you have handled the matter here, you are like to be cur'd of your madness.

Fra. And none but she can cure it.

Lol. Well, I'll give you over then, and she shall cast your water[273] next.

Fra. [*Giving him money*] Take for thy pains past.

Lol. I shall deserve more, sir, I hope; my mistress loves you, but must have some proof of your love to her.

Fra. There I meet my wishes.

Lol. That will not serve; you must meet her enemy and yours.

Fra. He's dead already.

Lol. Will you tell me that, and I parted but now with him?

Fra. Show me the man.

Lol. Ay, that's a right course now: see him before you kill him, in any case; and yet it needs not go so far neither: 'tis but a fool that haunts the house, and my mistress in the shape of an idiot. Bang but his fools' coat well-favouredly, and 'tis well.

Fra. Soundly, soundly.

Lol. Only reserve him till the masque be past; and if you find him not now in the dance yourself, I'll show you. In, in: my master!

Enter Alibius.

Fra. [*Dancing*] He handles him like a feather. Hey!

[*Exit.

Ali. Well said! In a readiness, Lollio?

Lol. Yes, sir.

---

[272]Steal.

[273]Diagnose your condition by examining your urine.

Ali. Away then, and guide them in, Lollio;
Entreat your mistress to see this sight.
Hark, is there not one incurable fool
That might be begg'd?[274] I have friends.

Lol. I have him for you, one that shall deserve it too.

Ali. Good boy, Lollio.

[Lollio *brings on the* Madmen *and* Fools. *The* Madmen *and* Fools *dance.*

'Tis perfect: well fit but once these strains,[275]
We shall have coin and credit for our pains.

[*Exeunt.*

---

[274]To beg a fool means to attempt to become someone's ward in order to enjoy his estate.
[275]Only prepare the music.

ACT V.

SCENE I.

A gallery in the castle.

Enter Beatrice. *A clock strikes one.*

Bea. One struck, and yet she lies by't. Oh, my fears,
This strumpet serves her own ends, 'tis apparent now,
Devours the pleasure with a greedy appetite,
And never minds my honour or my peace,
Makes havoc of my right; but she pays dearly for't:
No trusting of her life with such a secret,
That cannot rule her blood to keep her promise.
Beside, I have some suspicion of her faith to me,
Because I was suspected of my lord,
And it must come from her. Hark, by my horrors,
Another clock strikes two.

Strike two. Enter Deflores.

Def. Pist, where are you?

Bea. Deflores?

Def. Ay. Is she not come from him yet?

Bea. As I am a living soul, not.

Def. Sure the devil
Hath sow'd his itch within her; who'd trust
A waiting-woman?

Bea. I must trust somebody.

Def. Push, they are termagants.[276]
Especially when they fall upon their masters
And have their ladies' first fruits, th'are mad whelps;
You cannot stave 'em off[277] from game royal then.
You are so harsh and hardy, ask no counsel;
And I could have help'd you to an apothecary's daughter

---

[276]Fierce, shrewish women, from the name of god the Muslims were believed to have worshipped.

[277]A term to describe the method of holding dogs back at bear- and bull-baitings.

Would have fall'n off before eleven, and thank'd you too.

Bea. Oh me, not yet? This whore forgets herself.

Def. The rascal fares so well. Look, y'are undone:
The day-star, by this hand; see Phosphorus[278] plain yonder.

Bea. Advise me now to fall upon some ruin;[279]
There is no counsel safe else.

Def. Peace, I ha't now:
For we must force a rising;[280] there's no remedy.

Bea. How? Take heed of that.

Def. Tush, be you quiet
Or else give over all.

Bea. Prithee, I ha' done then.

Def. This is my reach: I'll set some part afire
Of Diaphanta's chamber.

Bea. How? Fire, sir?
That may endanger the whole house.

Def. You talk of danger when your fame's on fire?

Bea. That's true. Do what thou wilt now.

Def. Push, I aim
At a most rich success, strikes all dead sure.
The chimney being afire, and some light parcels
Of the least danger in her chamber only,
If Diaphanta should be met by chance then
Far from her lodging, which is now suspicious,
It would be thought her fears and affright then
Drove her to seek for succour; if not seen
Or met at all, as that's the likeliest,
For her own shame she'll hasten towards her lodging.
I will be ready with a piece[281] high-charg'd,

---

[278]The Morning-star.

[279]I.e., to devise a plot for Diaphanta's death.

[280]Wake the entire household.

[281]Birding-piece, gun.

As 'twere to cleanse the chimney: there, 'tis proper[282] now,
But she shall be the mark.

Bea. I'm forc'd to love thee now,
'Cause thou provid'st so carefully for my honour.

Def. 'Slid, it concerns the safety of us both,
Our pleasure and continuance.

Bea. One word now,
Prithee: how for the servants?

Def. I'll dispatch them,
Some one way, some another, in the hurry
For buckets, hooks, ladders. Fear not you;
The deed shall find its time, and I've thought since
Upon a safe conveyance for the body too.
How this fire purifies wit! Watch you your minute.

Bea. Fear keeps my soul upon't; I cannot stray from't.

Enter Alonzo's Ghost.

Def. Ha! What art thou that tak'st away the light
'Twixt that star and me? I dread thee not!
'Twas but a mist of conscience. All's clear again.

Exit Deflores.

Bea. Who's that, Deflores? Bless me! It slides by.

[*Exit* Ghost.

Some ill thing haunts the house; 't has left behind it
A shivering sweat upon me: I'm afraid now.
This night hath been so tedious. Oh, this strumpet!
Had she a thousand lives, he should not leave her
Till he had destroy'd the last.

Strikes three a' clock.

List! Oh, my terrors,
Three struck by St. Sebastian's!

[*Within*] Fire, fire, fire!

---

[282]Complete, ready for execution.

Bea. Already! How rare is that man's speed!
How heartily he serves me! His face loathes[283] one,
But look upon his care, who would not love him?
The east is not more beauteous than his service.

[*Within*]. Fire, fire, fire!

         Enter Deflores. Servants *pass over, ring a bell.*

Def. Away, dispatch!
Hooks, buckets, ladders; that's well said!
The fire bell rings, the chimney works, my charge:
The piece is ready.

                                             [*Exit.*

Bea. Here's a man worth loving!
Oh, y'are a jewel!

                     Enter Diaphanta.

Dia. Pardon frailty, madam;
In troth, I was so well, I ev'n forgot myself.

Bea. Y'have made trim work.

Dia. What?

Bea. Hie quickly to your chamber;
Your reward follows you.

Dia. I never made
So sweet a bargain.

                                             [*Exit.*

                     Enter Alsemero.

Als. Oh, my dear Joanna!
Alas, art thou risen too? I was coming,
My absolute treasure.

Bea. When I miss'd you,
I could not choose but follow.

Als. Th'art all sweetness.

---

[283]Disgusts.

80

The fire is not so dangerous.

Bea. Think you so, sir?

Als. I prithee, tremble not: believe me, 'tis not.

Enter Vermandero, Jasperino.

Ver. Oh, bless my house and me!

Als. My lord your father.

Enter Deflores *with a piece.*

Ver. Knave, whither goes that piece?

Def. To scour the chimney,

[*Exit.*

Ver. Oh, well said, well said;
That fellow's good on all occasions.

Bea. A wondrous necessary man, my lord.

Ver. He hath a ready wit; he's worth 'em all, sir:
Dog at a house on fire; I ha' seen him sing'd ere now.

The piece goes off.

Ha, there he goes!

Bea. 'Tis done.

Als. Come, sweet, to bed now;
Thou wilt get cold.

Bea. Alas, the fear keeps that out:
My heart will find no quiet till I hear
How Diaphanta, my poor woman, fares;
It is her chamber, sir, her lodging chamber.

Ver. How should the fire come there?

Bea. As good a soul as ever lady countenanc'd,[284]
But in her chamber negligent and heavy.

---

[284]Employed.

She scap'd a mine[285] twice.

Ver. Twice?

Bea. Strangely twice, sir.

Ver. Those sleepy sluts are dangerous in a house,
And they be ne'er so good.

Enter Deflores.

Def. Oh, poor virginity!
Thou hast paid dearly for't.

Ver. Bless us! What's that?

Def. A thing you all knew once: Diaphanta's burnt.

Bea. My woman, oh, my woman!

Def. Now the flames are
Greedy of her; burnt, burnt, burnt to death, sir.

Bea. Oh, my presaging soul!

Als. Not a tear more,
I charge you by the last embrace I gave you
In bed before this rais'd us.

Bea. Now you tie me;
Were it my sister now she gets no more.

Enter Servant.

Ver. How now?

Serv. All danger's past; you may now take
Your rests, my lords: the fire is throughly quench'd.
Ah, poor gentlewoman, how soon was she stifled!

Bea. Deflores, what is left of her inter,
And we as mourners all will follow her:
I will entreat that honour to my servant,
Ev'n of my lord himself.

Als. Command it, sweetness.

---

[285]A buried explosive, e.g. a contact mine, therefore an unspecified hidden danger.

Bea. Which of you spied the fire first?

Def. 'Twas I, madam.

Bea. And took such pains in't too? A double goodness!
'Twere well he were rewarded.

Ver. He shall be.
Deflores, call upon me.

Als. And upon me, sir.

[*Exeunt. Manet* Deflores.

Def. Rewarded? Precious, here's a trick beyond me;
I see in all bouts both of sport and wit
Always a woman strives for the last hit.

[*Exit.*

SCENE II.

A chamber.

Enter Tomazo.

Tom. I cannot taste the benefits of life
With the same relish I was wont to do.
Man I grow weary of, and hold his fellowship
A treacherous, bloody friendship, and because
I am ignorant in whom my wrath should settle,
I must think all men villains; and the next
I meet, whoe'er he be, the murderer
Of my most worthy brother.

Enter Deflores, *passes over the stage.*

Ha! What's he?
Oh, the fellow that some call honest Deflores;
But methinks honesty was hard bested
To come there for a lodging, as if a queen
Should make her palace of a pest-house.[286]
I find a contrariety in nature
Betwixt that face and me. The least occasion

---

[286]A house of pestilence, i.e., hospital for infectious diseases, especially plague.

83

Would give me game upon[287] him; yet he's so foul
One would scarce touch him with a sword he loved
And made account of.[288] So most deadly venomous,
He would go near to poison any weapon
That should draw blood on him; one must resolve
Never to use that sword again in fight
In way of honest manhood that strikes him.
Some river must devour 't; 'twere not fit
That any man should find it.

Enter Deflores.

What, again?
He walks a' purpose by, sure, to choke me up,
To infect my blood.

Def. My worthy noble lord.

Tom. Dost offer to come near and breath upon me?

[*Strikes him.*

Def. A blow.

[Deflores *draws his weapon.*

Tom. Yea, are you so prepar'd?
I'll rather like a soldier die by th' sword
Then like a politician[289] by thy poison.

Def. Hold, my lord, as you are honourable.

Tom. All slaves that kill by poison are still cowards.

Def. [*Aside*] I cannot strike: I see his brother's wounds
Fresh bleeding in his eye, as in a crystal.[290]--
I will not question this; I know y'are noble.
I take my injury with thanks given, sir,
Like a wise lawyer, and as a favour,
Will wear it for the worthy hand that gave it.
[*Aside*] Why this from him that yesterday appear'd

---

[287]Incite me to attack; to be in game = to be engaged in hunting.

[288]Valued.

[289]Schemer.

[290]Crystal ball.

84

So strangely loving to me? Oh, but instinct
Is of a subtler strain; guilt must not walk
So near his lodge again: he came near me now.

[Exit.

Tom. All league with mankind I renounce forever
Till I find this murderer. Not so much
As common courtesy but I'll lock up,
For in the state of ignorance I live in,
A brother may salute his brother's murderer,
And wish good speed to th' villain in a greeting.

Enter Vermandero, Alibius and Isabella.

Ver. Noble Piracquo.

Tom. Pray keep on your way, sir,
I've nothing to say to you.

Ver. Comforts bless you, sir.

Tom. I have forsworn complement,[291] in troth I have, sir;
As you are merely man, I have not left
A good wish for you, nor any here.

Ver. Unless you be so far in love with grief
You will not part from't upon any terms,
We bring that news will make a welcome for us.

Tom. What news can that be?

Ver. Throw no scornful smile
Upon the zeal I bring you, tis worth more, sir:
Two of the chiefest men I kept about me
I hide not from the law or your just vengeance.

Tom. Ha!

Ver. To give your peace more ample satisfaction,
Thank these discoverers.

Tom. If you bring that calm,
Name but the manner I shall ask forgiveness in
For that contemptuous smile upon you:

---

[291]Courtesy.

I'll perfect it with reverence that belongs
Unto a sacred altar.

[*Kneels.*

Ver. [*Raising him*] Good sir, rise,
Why, now you over-do as much a' this hand
As you fell short a' t'other. Speak, Alibius.

Ali. 'Twas my wife's fortune, as she is most lucky
At a discovery to find out lately
Within our hospital of fools and madmen
Two counterfeits slipp'd into these disguises,
Their names, Franciscus and Antonio.

Ver. Both mine, sir, and I ask no favour for 'em.

Ali. Now that which draws suspicion to their habits,
The time of their disguisings agrees justly
With the day of the murder.

Tom. Oh, blest revelation!

Ver. Nay more, nay more, sir, I'll not spare mine own
In way of justice: they both feign'd a journey
To Briamata, and so wrought out their leaves;[292]
My love was so abus'd in't.

Tom. Time's too precious
To run in waste now; you have brought a peace
The riches of five kingdoms could not purchase.
Be my most happy conduct. I thirst for 'em:
Like subtle lightning will I wind about 'em
And melt their marrow in 'em.[293]

[*Exeunt.*

SCENE III.

Alsemero's chamber.

Enter Alsemero *and* Jasperino.

---

[292]Cunningly obtained permission to leave.

[293]It was believed that lightning melted the marrow in the bones while leaving the rest of the body free from disfigurement.

86

Jas. Your confidence, I'm sure, is now of proof.
The prospect from the garden has show'd
Enough for deep suspicion.

Als. The black mask[294]
That so continually was worn upon't
Condemns the face for ugly ere 't be seen,
Her despite to him, and so seeming bottomless.

Jas. Touch it home[295] then; 'tis not a shallow probe
Can search this ulcer soundly: I fear you'll find it
Full of corruption. 'Tis fit I leave you.
She meets you opportunely from that walk;
She took the back door at his parting with her.

[*Exit* Jasperino.

Als. Did my fate wait for this unhappy stroke
At my first sight of woman?

Enter Beatrice.

She's here.

Bea. Alsemero!

Als. How do you?

Bea. How do I?
Alas! How do you? You look not well.

Als. You read me well enough; I am not well.

Bea. Not well, sir? Is't in my power to better you?

Als. Yes.

Bea. Nay, then y'are cur'd again.

Als. Pray resolve me one question, lady.

Bea. If I can.

---

[294]Beatrice's hypocrisy: i.e., her professed loathing of Deflores was a pretense to hide a sinister motive. Williams examines the following lines at length.

[295]Get to the bottom of it.

87

Als. None can so sure. Are you honest?[296]

Bea. Ha, ha, ha, that's a broad[297] question, my lord.

Als. But that's not a modest answer, my lady:
Do you laugh? My doubts are strong upon me

Bea. 'Tis innocence that smiles, and no rough brow
Can take away the dimple in her cheek.
Say I should strain a tear to fill the vault,[298]
Which would you give the better faith to?

Als. 'Twere but hypocrisy of a sadder[299] colour,
But the same stuff; neither your smiles nor tears
Shall move or flatter me from my belief:
You are a whore.

Bea. What a horrid sound it hath!
It blasts a beauty to deformity;
Upon what face soever that breath falls,
It strikes it ugly: oh, you have ruin'd
What you can ne'er repair again!

Als. I'll all demolish and seek out truth within you,
If there be any left: let your sweet tongue
Prevent[300] your heart's rifling; there I'll ransack
And tear out my suspicion.

Bea. You may, sir,
'Tis an easy passage; yet if you please,
Show me the ground whereon you lost your love.
My spotless virtue may but tread on that
Before I perish.

Als. Unanswerable;
A ground you cannot stand on: you fall down
Beneath all grace and goodness when you set

---

[296]Chaste.

[297]1) wide, 2) coarse.

[298]Heavens.

[299]Darker.

[300]Anticipate.

Your ticklish[301] heel on't. There was a visor[302]
O'er that cunning face, and that became you;
Now impudence[303] in triumph rides upon't.
How comes this tender reconcilement else
'Twixt you and your despite, your rancourous loathing,
Deflores? He that your eye was sore at sight of,
He's now become your arms' supporter,[304] your
Lips' saint.

Bea. Is there the cause?

Als. Worse: your lust's devil,
Your adultery.

Bea. Would any but yourself say that,
'Twould turn him to a villain.

Als. 'Twas witness'd
By the counsel of your bosom, Diaphanta.

Bea. Is your witness dead then?

Als. 'Tis to be fear'd
It was the wages of her knowledge, poor soul;
She liv'd not long after the discovery.

Bea. Then hear a story of not much less horror
Than this your false suspicion is beguil'd with.
To your bed's scandal I stand up innocence,[305]
Which even the guilt of one black other deed
Will stand for proof of: your love has made me
A cruel murderess.

Als. Ha!

Bea. A bloody one.
I have kiss'd poison for't, strok'd a serpent,
That thing of hate, worthy in my esteem

---

[301]Lascivious.

[302]Mask.

[303]Immodesty.

[304]1) i.e., holding her in an embrace, 2) an allusion to the figures who supported the family crest on a coat of arms, 3) possibly an ironic reference to Deflores being Beatrice's henchman.

[305]Plead innocence, as in a court of law; some editors emend to "innocent," but cf. *Antony and Cleopatra* I. i.

Of no better employment, and him most worthy
To be so employ'd I caus'd to murder
That innocent Piracquo, having no
Better means than that worst, to assure
Yourself to me.

Als. Oh, the place[306] itself e'er since
Has crying been for vengeance, the temple
Where blood and beauty first unlawfully
Fir'd their devotion and quench'd the right one.
'Twas in my fears at first: 'twill have it now.[307]
Oh, thou art all deform'd!

Bea. Forget not, sir,
It for your sake was done: shall greater dangers
Make the less welcome?

Als. Oh, thou shouldst have gone
A thousand leagues about to have avoided
This dangerous bridge of blood; here we are lost.

Bea. Remember I am true unto your bed.

Als. The bed itself's a charnel,[308] the sheets shrouds
For murdered carcasses; it must ask pause
What I must do in this. Meantime you shall
Be my prisoner only; enter my closet.

                                        [*Exit* Beatrice.

I'll be your keeper yet. Oh, in what part
Of this sad story shall I first begin?

                    Enter Deflores.

Ha! This same fellow has put me in.[309]
Deflores.

Def. Noble Alsemero!

Als. I can tell you

---

[306]The temple.
[307]I.e., the temple will have its vengeance.
[308]A vault for the remains of the dead.
[309]Give me the idea (where to begin).

News, sir: my wife has her commended to you.

Def. That's news indeed, my lord; I think she would
Commend me to the gallows if she could,
She ever lov'd me so well. I thank her.

Als. What's this blood upon your band,[310] Deflores?

Def. Blood? No, sure 'twas wash'd since.

Als. Since when, man?

Def. Since t'other day I got a knock
In a sword and dagger school; I think 'tis out.

Als. Yes, 'tis almost out, but 'tis perceiv'd, though.
I had forgot my message; this it is:
What price goes murder?

Def. How, sir?

Als. I ask you, sir:
My wife's behindhand[311] with you, she tells me,
For a brave, bloody blow you gave for her sake
Upon Piracquo.

Def. Upon? 'Twas quite through him, sure.
Has she confess'd it?

Als. As sure as death to both of you,
And much more than that.

Def. It could not be much more;
'Twas but one thing, and that she's a whore.

Als. It could not choose but follow. Oh, cunning devils!
How should blind men know you from fair-fac'd saints?

Bea. [*within*] He lies, the villain does belie me!

Def. Let me go to her, sir.

Als. Nay, you shall to her.
Peace, crying crocodile, your sounds are heard;
Take your prey to you! Get you into her, sir.

---

[310]Collar.
[311]Indebted to.

Exit Deflores.

I'll be your pander now; rehearse again
Your scene of lust, that you may be perfect
When you shall come to act it to the black audience[312]
Where howls and gnashings shall be music to you.
Clip[313] your adulteress freely; 'tis the pilot
Will guide you to the *Mare Mortuum*,
Where you shall sink to fathoms bottomless.

Enter Vermandero, Alibius, Isabella, Tomazo, Franciscus, *and* Antonio.

Ver. Oh, Alsemero. I have a wonder for you.

Als. No, sir, 'tis I, I have a wonder for you.

Ver. I have suspicion near as proof itself
For Piracquo's murder.

Als. Sir, I have proof
Beyond suspicion for Piracquo's murder.

Ver. Beseech you hear me: these two have been disguis'd
E'er since the deed was done.

Als. I have two other
That were more close disguis'd then your two could be,
E'er since the deed was done.

Ver. You'll hear me: these mine own servants--

Als. Hear me: those nearer than your servants
That shall acquit them and prove them guiltless.

Fra. That may be done with easy truth, sir.

Tom. How is my cause bandied[314] through your delays!
'Tis urgent in blood, and calls for haste;
Give me a brother alive or dead:
Alive, a wife with him; if dead, for both
A recompense for murder and adultery.[315]

Bea. [*within*] Oh, oh, oh!

---

[312]Devils; Daalder cites Matthew 13.42, "wailing and gnashing of teeth".

[313]Embrace.

[314]Tossed back and forth.

92

Als. Hark, 'tis coming to you.

Def. [*within*] Nay, I'll along for company.

Bea. [*within*] Oh, oh!

Ver. What horrid sounds are these?

Als. Come forth, you twins of mischief.

Enter Deflores *bringing in* Beatrice *wounded.*

Def. Here we are; if you have any more
To say to us, speak quickly. I shall not
Give you the hearing else; I am so stout yet,
And so, I think, that broken rib of mankind.[316]

Ver. An host of enemies entered my citadel
Could not amaze like this. Joanna, Beatrice Joanna!

Bea. Oh, come not near me, sir; I shall defile you.
I am that of your blood was taken from you
For your better health;[317] look no more upon't,
But cast it to the ground regardlessly:
Let the common sewer take it from distinction.[318]
Beneath the stars, upon yon meteor[319]
Ever hung my fate, 'mongst things corruptible;
I ne'er could pluck it from him. My loathing
Was prophet to the rest but ne'er believ'd;
Mine honour fell with him, and now my life.
Alsemero, I am a stranger to your bed;
Your bed was coz'ned on the nuptial night,
For which your false bride died.

Als. Diaphanta!

---

[315]Tomazo regards Beatrice's marriage to Alsemero as adultery because she was betrothed to Alonzo first. (He is not referring to her adultery with Deflores against Alsemero, which Tomazo could not know about).

[316]I.e., Beatrice, alluding to Eve having been created from Adam's rib.

[317]I.e., Vermandero has undergone blood-letting, Beatrice being the infected blood.

[318]State of being distinct, i.e., let it become mixed with the sewage.

[319]The meteor she refers to is Deflores. According to medieval astrology, the stars that controlled men's fate (cf. "star-crossed lovers") were fixed and incorruptible; on the other hand, meteors, which were sublunary, were corruptible and subject to change, and heralded or were provoked by evil events on earth. Cf. *Julius Caesar* I. iii & II. i.

Def. Yes, and the while I coupled with your mate
At barley-break; now we are left in hell.

Ver. We are all there; it circumscribes us[320] here.

Def. I lov'd this woman in spite of her heart;
Her love I earn'd out of Piracquo's murder.

Tom. Ha, my brother's murderer!

Def. Yes, and her honour's prize
Was my reward; I thank life for nothing
But that pleasure: it was so sweet to me
That I have drunk up all, left none behind
For any man to pledge me.

Ver. Horrid villain!
Keep life in him for further tortures.

Def. No,
I can prevent you; here's my penknife still.
It is but one thread more, [*stabbing himself*] and now 'tis cut.
Make haste, Joanna, by that token[321] to thee:
Canst not forget, so lately put in mind,
I would not go to leave thee far behind.

[*Dies.*

Bea. Forgive me, Alsemero, all forgive;
'Tis time to die when 'tis a shame to live.

[*Dies.*

Ver. Oh, my name is entered now in that record[322]
Where till this fatal hour 'twas never read!

Als. Let it be blotted out; let your heart lose it,
And it can never look you in the face,
Nor tell a tale behind the back of life
To your dishonour. Justice hath so right
The guilty hit, that innocence is quit

---

[320]Cf. the note above on barley-break; there is an echo of Marlowe's *Dr. Faustus* II. i.
[321]Either his wound or (most likely) the wound he gave her; her not being able to forget it alludes to the nature of love tokens as forget-me-nots.
[322]The heavenly record of misdeeds.

By proclamation,[323] and may joy again.
Sir, you are sensible of what truth hath done;
'Tis the best comfort that your grief can find.

Tom. Sir, I am satisfied; my injuries
Lie dead before me. I can exact no more,
Unless my soul were loose and could o'ertake
Those black fugitives[324] that are fled from thence
To take a second vengeance; but there are wraths
Deeper than mine, 'tis to be fear'd, about 'em.

Als. What an opacous[325] body had that moon
That last chang'd on us! Here's beauty chang'd
To ugly whoredom, here servant obedience
To a master sin, imperious murder.
I, a suppos'd husband, chang'd embraces
With wantonness, but that was paid before;[326]
Your change is come too, from an ignorant wrath
To knowing friendship. Are there any more on's?

Ant. Yes, sir, I was chang'd too, from a little ass as I was to a great fool
as I am; and had like to ha' been chang'd to the gallows but that you
know my innocence[327] always excuses me.

Fra. I was chang'd from a little wit to be stark mad, almost for the same
purpose.

Isa. [*To Alibius*] Your change is still behind,
But deserve best your transformation.
You are a jealous coxcomb, keep schools of folly,
And teach your scholars how to break your own head.[328]

Ali. I see all apparent, wife, and will change now
Into a better husband, and never keep scholars
That shall be wiser then myself.

Als. Sir, you have yet a son's duty living;
Please you accept it. Let that your sorrow,

---

[323]Acquitted by a public proclamation of the truth.

[324]The souls of Beatrice and Deflores on their way to hell.

[325]Opaque, darkened, and therefore ominous.

[326]I.e., Diaphanta paid with her life.

[327]1) guiltlessness, 2) idiocy or "lunacy," being in the grip of love.

[328]I.e., with cuckold's horns.

As it goes from your eye, go from your heart;
Man and his sorrow at the grave must part.

EPILOGUE.

Als. All we can do to comfort one another,
To stay[329] a brother's sorrow for a brother,
To dry a child from the kind father's eyes,
Is to no purpose; it rather multiplies.
Your only smiles have power to cause relive
The dead again, or in their rooms to give
Brother a new brother, father a child:
If these appear, all griefs are reconcil'd.

[*Exeunt omnes.*

---

[329]Stop.

Made in the USA
San Bernardino, CA
26 August 2019